TAILS OF SCOTLAND
The Story of Scottish Dogs

Peter MacQueen

Black&White

Black&White

First published in the UK in 2025 by Black & White Publishing
An imprint of Bonnier Books UK
5th Floor, HYLO, 105 Bunhill Row, London, EC1Y 8LZ

Copyright © Peter MacQueen 2025
Photography credits listed on page 250

All rights reserved.
No part of this publication may be reproduced, stored or transmitted in any form by any means, electronic, mechanical, photocopying or otherwise, without the prior written permission of the publisher.

The right of Peter MacQueen to be identified as Author of this work has been asserted by him in accordance with the Copyright, Designs and Patents Act, 1988.

The publisher has made every reasonable effort to contact copyright holders of images in this book. Any errors are inadvertent and anyone who for any reason has not been contacted is invited to write to the publisher so that a full acknowledgement can be made in subsequent editions of this work.

A CIP catalogue record for this book is available from the British Library.

ISBN: 978 1 78530 848 2

1 3 5 7 9 10 8 6 4 2

Layout by Richard Budd
Printed and bound in Lithuania

The authorised representative in the EEA is Bonnier Books UK (Ireland) Limited.
Registered office address: Floor 3, Block 3, Miesian Plaza, Dublin 2, D02 Y754, Ireland
compliance@bonnierbooks.ie

www.bonnierbooks.co.uk

For Coinneach
The leader of our wee pack –
tha gaol agam ort

CONTENTS

Introduction	2
Bringing a Puppy Home	8
1. The Scottish Deerhound	15
2. The Cairn Terrier	31
3. The Skye Terrier	45
4. The West Highland White Terrier	63
5. The Scottish Terrier	77
6. The Dandie Dinmont Terrier	93
7. The Border Terrier	109
8. The Gordon Setter	123
9. The Bearded Collie	139
10. The Rough Collie	155
11. The Smooth Collie	169
12. The Shetland Sheepdog	183
13. The Border Collie	195
14. The Golden Retriever	211
The Hebridean Baker's Oaty Dog Biscuits	229
Feeding as Nature Intended	231
Teach Your Dog Scotland's Languages	236
Scottish Names For Your Dog	239
Scotland's Dogs on Show	242
Scotland's Breed Clubs & Associations	248
A Hundred Thousand Thanks	249
About the Author	250

INTRODUCTION
Scotland – A Place of Many Paws

There are places in the world where dogs seem to belong more than people. Where they fit the land not just in form, but in feeling. Scotland as a place is very much of this ilk.

Walk any stretch of glen, shore, moor or machair and you'll find them – not just dogs, but *our* dogs. Bred for this land, shaped by it and part of its story, all of them carry something ancient, something majestic, and are fearless to the bone. They are weatherproof, sharp-witted, gritty and affectionate. Some bound across the heather with the energy of a Highland fling in their hearts, others curl under the kitchen table in a croft house – slumbering but alert, half watching with sleepy eyes waiting for the action to start.

This book is a celebration of those dogs – and for a small country, Scotland has a remarkable number to her name. Fourteen native breeds survive, each with a chapter of its own, each a living thread in the long weave of Scottish tweedy history. You'll meet the shaggy shepherds of the pastures and the whip-smart workers of the hills. The dignified hunters of old courts and the scrappy terriers who once kept farms and barns mouse free and lively with their presence. Some are familiar faces; others, sadly, a rarer affair. But all have shaped the lives, landscapes and loyalties of this country in ways that are too often overlooked.

This is not a dog encyclopaedia. Not a how-to manual, not a breeder's handbook, nor a treatise on dog show conformation points. It's much more like a love letter. More of a field guide to belonging and connection; a collection of stories about the canines of Caledonia and the people who love them.

For me, that love runs deep. Dogs have been a constant in my life. Their integrity, company, comedy, charm and occasional chaos have steadied me more times than I can count. I'm not entirely sure where I'd be without the hullaballoo they bring to brighten each day. And it was that precious bond which inspired me to embark upon this project in the first place.

Because if there's one truth that shines through these pages, it's this: dogs don't just walk beside us. They keep us on course through joy, through grief, through change. They dig us out when we're buried too deep, and they hold the line when everything else gives way. It is us who are collared by their faithful affection.

Every one of these dogs is real, and each story comes from real life. Some will make you laugh; some may well make you cry. You'll meet dogs who are companion dogs, rescue dogs, working dogs and show dogs – each one with a waggety tail and a heart like a TARDIS: impossibly big on the inside.

In telling their stories, I hope to honour not only the dogs themselves, but the people who live alongside them – the breeders, fosterers, farmers and friends. The unsung keepers of lines and

legacies, the good folk who hold fast to something more enduring than fashion or fad, which is so deeply embedded in the psyche of our nation.

So, dear reader, if a new dog for your home is on your mind, then everyone who's been part of the creation of this book has a simple recommendation for you – consider a Scottish breed. You won't regret it.

Fàilte a charaid – come away in. Wipe your boots. Mind the snoozing terrier by the fire and turn the page. The dogs of Scotland await.

ME AND MY DOGS

From what you've read so far, you'll know how much dogs matter to me. But allow me to gather the pack and introduce you properly. If this book is a love letter to Scotland's dogs, then these few pages are my own tribute to the ones who've shared my hearth, my adventures and my heart.

Let's begin with Peigi, our pepper-coloured Dandie Dinmont terrier. She's a year old as I write this, and a sturdy wee tank of a dog – funny, loving, a bit licky and full of sass. I belong to her, not the other way round, and she knows it. She's headstrong, gorgeous and utterly magnetic. Peigi's not just my dog – she's the boss of the entire MacQueen clan. Uncle Stuart is obsessed with her, lifting her up like a favourite niece. Graham, our resident bodach (my dad), plays it cool, but has been spotted more than once snuggling her in his favourite chair. Even my mum has been reeled in by those big doting eyes. When she sees my brothers Mark and Robin arriving at the house with their families, Peigi squeals with joy. She is a social superstar – especially with children.

Despite her dinky stature, Peigi is not a lapdog. She's a big dog on wee pins – swift, strong, surprisingly athletic and all instinct when she's outdoors. You can see how her breed once held its own against badgers and rats. Dandies are on the vulnerable rare breed list, a fact I honestly find baffling, as they make fantastic family dogs. Everyone who meets one falls head over heels. Indeed, it was my friend Ceitidh's Dandie, Machair, who first sparked my interest in this special breed, so charmed was I. My advice to anyone thinking about getting a dog is this – go out and meet lots of different dogs. You never know which one might spark something unexpected.

Now, to Flòraidh, our West Highland white terrier and the darling of the household. She had mighty paws to match, as you'll soon learn, but she's made her own mark with gentleness, loyalty and a cheerfulness that could brighten any grey day. She and Peigi are chalk and cheese as terriers, but they've become a right pair – my mismatched set of wee wally dugs. They get on beautifully; it's Peigi who leads the charge, but Flòraidh keeps a calm eye on the whole operation.

I came across them both when I had the great privilege of presenting a series for BBC Alba called Cù Leis Thu? – A Puppy for Pàdruig. When Claire the producer called to pitch the idea of me spending a summer travelling around Scotland meeting puppies, my tail was already wagging. It turned out to be one of the best gigs of my life. The joy of it, aside from the canine cuddles and road trips, was that it opened my heart again to the world of different breeds. For a long time, I had been a "Westie person", but my old boy had passed away the previous year. Before him, I had it in my head that I was a "collie man". Why do we do that – fixate on one type? Is it a way of grounding our identity, or simply a habit?

During my years at college in Skye, then university in Aberdeen and later at my first job with the BBC Gàidhlig department, it was just not practical for me to have dogs. Yet I still thought of myself as that "collie man", but then along came

my wee knight in white – Seòras the Westie.

Seòras was my heart dog. A West Highland white terrier, the runt of a litter I met on a farm in Ayrshire. When I couldn't choose between the three pups, Seòras made the choice for me, marching up to me and nudging my leg with purpose as if to say, "Mon then – mach à seo leinn." From that moment onwards, we were inseparable.

I was thirty-two when I brought him home, and for fifteen fabulous years he was my constant – it was an honour and a privilege to have been in his firmament. We climbed hills, wandered beaches, sat together in pubs, explored the islands, the mountains and the cities of Scotland, shared long drives, early mornings and daft nights. He came to work with me, charming the whole office and (conveniently) hoovering up any dropped sandwich crumbs. Speaking of hoovers, it was his arch enemy – hilariously, he would find the dust-busting device in any new place we visited and stare it out with great suspicion and anticipation! He even travelled with me to Rio de Janeiro when I moved there. Every morning he would trot along Copacabana beach, splashing merrily in the sea, sniffing out coconuts and, occasionally, puffer fish thrown up onto the sand by the tide. The local children adored him. He even changed his bark! Brazilian kids don't say "woof-woof", they say "ow-ow" – and Seòras eventually echoed this in tandem with my own Portuguese language skills.

I became known in the neighbourhood as O Escocês (the Scotsman), and the local delivery man would whizz by on his bike calling "Bom dia, Seòrasinho!" We later returned to Scotland and moved to the Isle of Lewis, where I worked at MacTV, and Seòras resumed his role as office dog and local celebrity. We'd stop each morning at Gress beach, where he'd run wild in the Hebridean breeze, snuffling the dunes or dancing the rippled sands, with his reflection paddy-baa-ing below his wet paws. At the office, he was greeted with affection – especially

by Peigi in accounts – "Madainn mhath a Sheòrais bhig" – and would snooze under desks while collecting ear rubs and contraband biscuits.

The first time Seòras met my partner, Coinneach, was on a canoe trip to our hut. I was worried about how we'd manage the boat and gave Coinneach clear instructions: if we capsize, you swim to shore and I'll get the dog. He later joked that our hierarchy was crystal clear. Seòras first. Always.

Before Seòras, there were others. Tanya, a rescue Great Dane, gifted to the family by an Oban hotelier when my brothers and I were still in nappies. Then Jack Russells named Penny and Mickey. My cousin Rhona had a Cairn called Sìthean and later a Border terrier called Cara whom I loved deeply too. But mostly, we had collies.

My childhood dog was Socks, a super smart Border collie I got from Alison at Achnalarig, just across the glen. I used to visit her dogs daily, and when they had a litter, I knew I wanted the little guy with the brown specks above his eyes. Knowing my parents would say no, I simply brought him home unannounced.

Mum tried to be the voice of reason and insist on "no". But even as she did, Dad was already down on the floor cuddling the little scamp. On her third

attempt at saying, "No way, Jose," we were all laughing and the puppy had leapt up onto Mum's knee to kiss her nose. And that, as they say, was that.

So yes, I once thought I was a collie man, and then a Westie guy – but isn't that the beauty of dogs? They shift your perspective. They open doors, change minds and plant new loves in your life. If you think you know which dog is for you, I say this with great affection: keep your heart open. You never know which muddy-pawed marvel will waddle in and turn your world upside down.

And, especially, keep your mind open to the Scottish breeds. They have walked with us through the ages, and they need us now more than ever.

BRINGING A PUPPY HOME
The Day Everything Changes

The day we brought Flòraidh home, the house changed shape.

It had been about eight months since Seòras passed – long enough for the quiet to settle in, but not so long that it stopped feeling strange. We'd always had dogs around, so that silence had become the loudest thing in the room. For us, it's simple: a house is not a home without dogs. Some of you, I know, will prefer to adopt an older dog, and there are brilliant organisations dedicated to the rehoming of native Scottish breeds. Giving a new start to a dog in need is every bit as joyous as welcoming a new pup.

Like Seòras, Flòraidh was a Westie, bold as brass and, on that day, barely bigger than the size of my palm. She marched in like she owned the place, tail high, ears pricked, already poking her nose into every corner. That first evening she curled up on my foot like she'd always been there, and I remember thinking that the house felt right again: like home.

A few weeks later, Peigi arrived, our bonnie Dandie Dinmont terrier. Quieter at first, more considered, she stepped into the house with the gravity of someone who meant to stay. Tiny, wiry and wise – an old soul in a pup's body – she had a bark like a cracked bell and great dark eyes that seemed to ask questions you didn't quite know how to answer.

Those early days were equal parts joy and disarray. Boots mysteriously relocated, jackets chewed and a fair few midnight wanderings in the rain. But also tiny snores from under the chair, the tentative press of a furry head into your hand, the flicker of recognition when they heard their name. A kind of soft alchemy had begun.

Bringing home a pup, especially one of Scotland's own, is never just about the dog. It's about returning to a different routine, laughter, muddy floors

and chewed socks. For me, it was about re-finding the version of myself that only dogs can see.

PREPARING THE SPACE

Before the pup sets paw inside, you'll want to make the place feel ready. A blanket from the breeder – still carrying the scent of mum and siblings – can ease the transition more than any gadget from the pet shop. Set up a soft bed in a quiet corner, away from clatter and clang. Somewhere warm, cosy and safe where they can tuck themselves away if need be. Every dog deserves a den.

You'll need two bowls (one for food, one for water), a collar and lead, poo bags and food that matches what the breeder fed them. Don't be swayed by posh packaging. Simply stick to what's familiar for the first few weeks – there'll be time enough for seaweed supplements and artisanal, hand-rolled kibble later.

And let's not pretend otherwise – puppies chew. Everything. Skirting boards, broom handles, fancy table legs. If it's wooden and beloved, it's fair game and they'll likely have a nibble. My advice? Offer plenty of tough chews, rotate them to keep interest high and

remove temptation wherever you can. They're only wee for a few weeks, so put the heirlooms away!

If you've got outdoor space, properly check your fences. Terriers, especially, are escape artists by instinct and inclination. If there's a gap the size of a buttered scone, they'll find it and be halfway to Inverness before you've laced your boots to give chase.

THE FIRST FORTY-EIGHT HOURS
Expect Very Little Sleep

Some pups cry through the night, missing their littermates. Others march in like lairds and fall asleep on your chest without a second thought – and both are normal responses. Try to keep things calm, so no parades of visiting admirers just yet. A warm water bottle (wrapped safely), a ticking clock or even the hum of *A' Mire ri Mòir* on Radio nan Gàidheal can help mimic the comfort of the pup's original nest.

Introduce other pets gently and, if possible, on neutral ground. Let the new arrival explore at their own pace. And if you've got a cat, hens or a hamster, don't expect pastoral harmony from day one. Remember, it takes time for a new addition to learn the rhythms of your household.

Above all, remember they're tiny, a wee bit confused and utterly dependent.

Patience will be your best friend. That and kitchen roll!

ROUTINE & RHYTHM

Dogs – especially Scotland's working and companion breeds – thrive on routine. Set feeding times and stick to them. Most breeders recommend four small meals a day for puppies at first, tapering down as they grow.

Toilet training is a matter of vigilance and reward. Take them out after waking, after eating and any time they start sniffing the floor like a truffle pig. Praise quietly – there's no need to clap like a game show host. Accidents will happen, but your job is just to clean up the bùrach without fuss and move on. Try not to let the pup start thinking of the tidy-up as a game – they will if you let them.

Nights can be tricky. Some folks swear by crate training, others by shared sleep. Find what suits your household, but avoid long periods of isolation. A pup isn't a parcel to be stored until morning; they need reassurance, presence and that low murmur of human life.

Those early days are when you begin building something magical. Say their name often, gently. Sit together. Let them learn your smell, your voice, your shape in the dark. Trust grows in these moments. And, for all of us, trust is where a relationship is made.

BUILDING TRUST, NOT JUST OBEDIENCE

In those early weeks, it's tempting to focus on the basics – *suidh sìos, fuirich, leig às* – or *sit doon, bide, drap it*. (Of course, you can speak English, or any other tongue, with your pup too.) Trust doesn't come from commands – it comes from what happens between them.

Let it build slowly, in the small stuff, the way they follow you from room to room, even when nothing's happening. The pause before they cross a threshold, waiting for your nod. The slow tail wag when they see you stir.

I remember fixing a strip of fencing one morning, muttering at the cold wire. Peigi, still only a pup, didn't dash off or dig. She sat nearby and watched, blinking at me – not waiting for a biscuit, just content being there. That's when I knew we were beginning to know each other – not through commands, but through presence.

COMMUNITY & CULTURE

Where you find good dogs, you'll often find good people. Buying from a reputable breeder or finding a rehoming centre means not just proper health checks and paperwork, but someone to call when things get confusing. Avoid anonymous listings – a real breeder worth their salt will want to know you, and be known by you.

Once your pup's jabs are done, get them out into the world. Scottish breeds were made for adventure, so you can enjoy familiarising them with their environment – go up braes, along the shore or down the lane. Visit the village shop. Stay for the craic in a dog-friendly pub. Stop at your local park and chat to the dog folk there. Or let them feel the sea air on a gentle ferry crossing. And seriously – has anyone ever been to a good house cèilidh that *didn't* have a dog or two making the rounds?

The world is your dog's classroom, but be mindful of others while your pup is still learning. Not everyone will appreciate the phrase "they're only a puppy". Through socialisation, patience and perseverance, your pup becomes more than your pet. They become a familiar face at the post office, a magnet for a blether at the garden gate and a comfort to elderly neighbours who may no longer bend so easily to pat them, but who still smile when they see one. Dogs form part of community, so join in.

A FINAL NOTE – THE HEART OPENS

There's a magic to raising a dog – a kind of hope you don't quite realise you've been carrying until you see them asleep in their basket with wee paws twitching as they chase rabbits in their dreams. With a steady hand, a warm space, a voice that speaks kindly, they thrive. Dogs can't help but give 100 per cent, which is what they deserve in return.

One day, you'll look up and realise the pup you brought home that day all those years ago has grown grey around the muzzle. But just now, they're new and the world outside awaits them. And you – lucky soul! – you're at the beginning of the best years, so trust the process. It might stretch you at times, but your life will evolve and expand to accommodate their four-legged needs.

So breathe in the mischief of the early doggy days, the squeaky toys and the toothy yawns. You're doing more than getting a dog – you're becoming part of a story as full of love as a wee wet black button nose.

If your heart says yes to a puppy – and you're sure your home life, your pocket and your time can hold that choice – then trust it. They'll test you, yes. But their love will floor you. Scotland's native breeds need kind, committed homes. Which one sings to your soul, suits your lifestyle and brings a smile to your face? You won't regret the time they share on this earth with you.

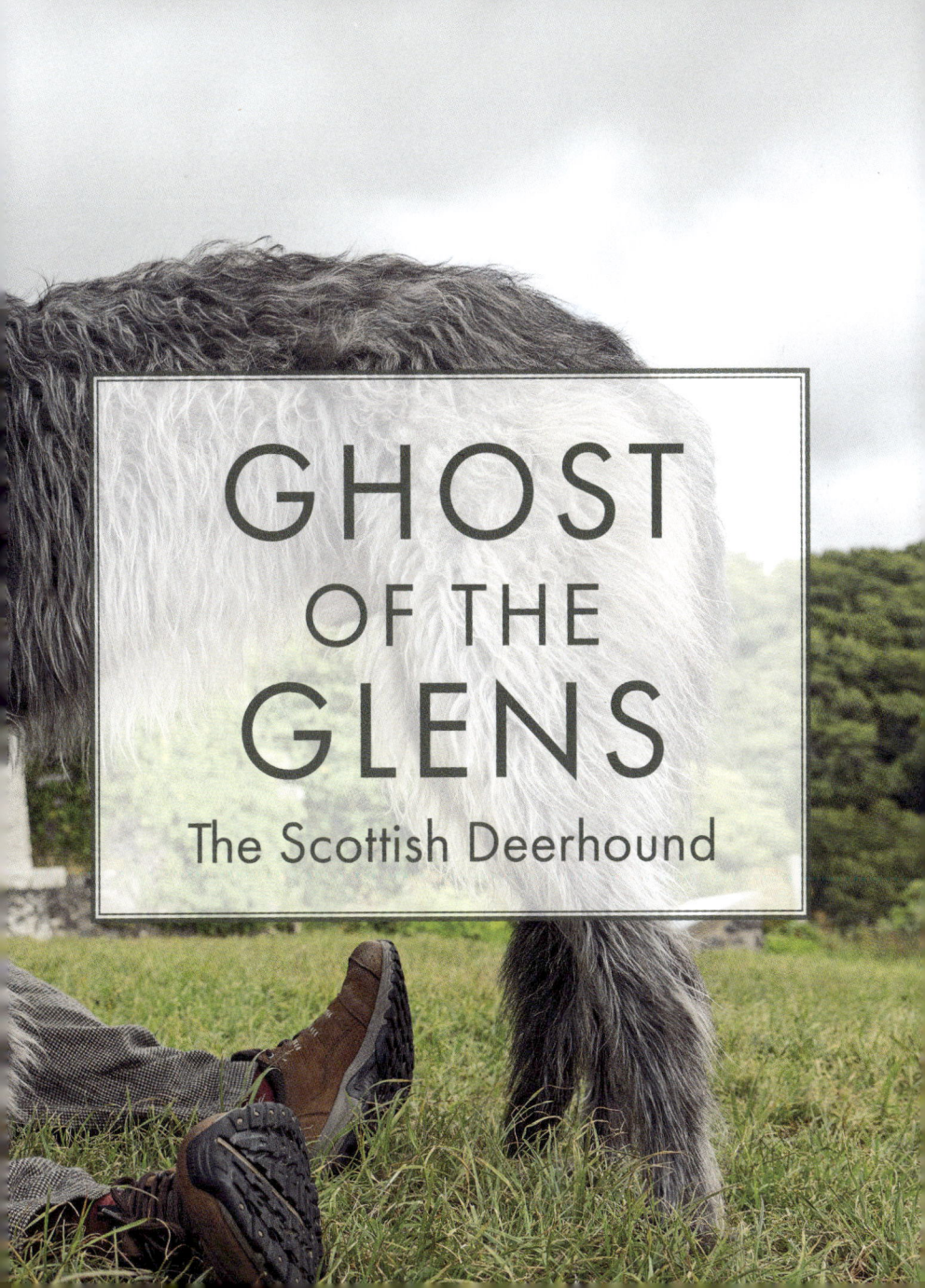

BREED STANDARD

GENERAL APPEARANCE: Resembles a rough-coated greyhound of larger size and bone.
COAT: Harsh and wiry at 8–10 cm long.
COLOUR: Dark blue-grey preferred; also brindle, fawn, red fawn, grey.
EYES: Dark, soft in repose, keen when alert.
MOVEMENT: Easy, active and true with a long stride.
TEMPERAMENT: Gentle, friendly, dignified, eager to please.

THE NOBLE FORM

Tall as a stag's shoulder, elegant in their roguishness, the Scottish deerhound is unmistakable. Standing well over seventy centimetres at the withers, it has the look of a longer, leggier greyhound in a rough coat and dressed for Highland weather – strong-boned, deep-chested and built for the chase.

Its wiry hair is a weatherproof layer, with a slightly harsh texture and often in colours that mirror the heather – grey, blue-grey, brindle, fawn and red fawn. Red-coated deerhounds are not a separate variety, just a quirk of genetics that can make them seem taller or finer in frame. Its head is long and refined, with dark eyes full of feeling and the sudden spark of playfulness.

But it's their movement that leaves the deepest impression. A deerhound moves like it remembers something more ancient than the ground beneath it – there is no hurry, no tension. Just a stride as smooth and elegant as a river, even when loping over tussocky ground. They are unfathomably fast, truly built for the terrain of a Scottish wilderness.

Then there's the gaze. When a deerhound looks you in the eye, you know you've met a creature that understands the world. There's something almost mystical there – soulful, still and unforced. A sighthound's eyes don't just see, they connect. The deerhound's gaze can stop you in your tracks, as if it were looking not only at you, but *into* you – it is the uncanny feeling of being truly seen, as though your soul were briefly laid bare.

They are affectionate dogs, deeply so. And when one leans against you, as they so often do, it's not a nudge for attention, it's the deerhound lean – a sign you've been accepted into their world, and it can feel like the most humbling experience; their trusting acknowledgement is an honour indeed.

TEMPERAMENT – STILL & TRUE

Scottish deerhounds are sometimes called "the politest of dogs", and as anyone who knows them will testify, there's truth in it. They are courteous and soft-spoken; theirs is the presence that steadies a room.

With their humans, they are delightfully close: they lean, they sigh, they nuzzle with those long noses of theirs for a scratch between the ears. They might follow you about, not because they're anxious, but because they enjoy the comfort of shared company. And they're famously good with children, with other dogs and with guests – provided no one startles them mid-nap. Although often stoic, they are also ever ready for a bit of nonsense. You should see them trying to catch any unfortunate flies that enter

GROUP: Sighthound.
STATUS: Vulnerable.
ORIGIN: Earlier, the breed was known as the Scottish wolfdog, though its precise foundation stock has been lost to time. Lighter in frame than their closest kin, the Irish wolfhound, these grand dogs are tall and fleet, descending from ancient lines of Celtic sighthounds.
HEIGHT: Male: 76 cm. Female: 71cm. Minimum at the withers.
WEIGHT: Male: About 45.5 kg. Female: About 36.5 kg.

The Scottish Deerhound

their orbit and annoy them – cue the *snap, snap, snap* of jaws!

Like all sighthounds, they're not great watchdogs. They're unlikely to bark at the postie or challenge unexpected company or noise, but should danger come close, a deerhound's size and presence are a statement in themselves.

They're intelligent, but not slavishly obedient – more likely to weigh your request than obey it blindly. If I had to describe them in a single sentence, I'd say they're empathetic, occasionally aloof, sometimes a bit goofy – gentle, lanky, lazy and speedy giants with the kindest of hearts.

EXERCISE, SPACE & SLOWNESS

Deerhounds need room to stretch – a good run in a safe space a few times a week is ideal. But they're not frantic or restless. In fact, as with greyhounds, they tend to be "forty-mile-an-hour couch potatoes".

And it's true, they can reach top speeds of around 35 to 40 mph when in full sprint, though they save this ability for joyful bursts. (A word of warning: don't encourage one to build up speed if you're holding the lead – you may as well attach yourself to an accelerating Ferrari.) They'll chase if they catch a glimpse of sudden movement – that's the sighthound in them, so be careful around cats, rabbits, squirrels and so on, but indoors they're like moving sculptures: composed, poised and very likely draped across the furniture.

Deerhounds are not city dogs by nature – not because of their temperament, but because of their scale. In a small apartment, they can seem like a sideboard with opinions. But on a farm or in a home with easy access to a big garden and parks, they fit like poetry.

GROOMING & CARE

The coat, though rough-looking, is low-maintenance. A weekly brush – more often during moulting (yes they do moult, but not heavily in comparison to other breeds) – keeps it healthy and free of debris. Deerhounds don't have that classic doggy smell and they rarely need bathing unless they find something unspeakable to roll in.

Like many deep-chested breeds, they can be prone to bloat (gastric torsion) – a life-threatening condition requiring awareness and careful feeding routines, which means no exercise immediately after meals, smaller portions and raised bowls.

They can also be predisposed to bone cancer (osteosarcoma) more than some other breeds – a painful reality that breeders and researchers continue to study. While there is no guaranteed prevention, maintaining a healthy weight, providing low-impact exercise and sourcing from reputable breeders who screen their lines can reduce risk.

Like most larger breeds of dog, deerhounds tend to have a shorter lifespan; in their case, between eight and eleven years. This is, not always but often, part of the deal with these gentle giants, which is surely all the more reason to love them well if you are blessed to have one in your life. Still, many deerhounds live full, healthy lives with proper care. You'll find that they age with grace, wearing their wisdom in silvery fortitude and with great conviction.

DID YOU KNOW? DEERHOUND TRIVIA

- **What's in a Name?:** They were historically used to hunt red deer in the Highlands; hence their name.
- **Noble Connections:** The deerhound was a status symbol among Scottish lords, as ownership of these regal creatures was once restricted to nobility only.
- **Fighting Extinction:** The breed nearly disappeared more than once, most recently in the twentieth century.
- **For the Love of Sighthound:** These dogs are sighthounds: they hunt by vision and speed rather than scent.
- **Star Power!** They have famously appeared in film and TV, including *Outlander* and *The Queen*.
- **Turbocharged or Lazybones?** Despite their size, they are incredibly gentle indoors and like their greyhound cousins can be very "nonchalant" when off-duty.

TAILS IN THE TOPOGRAPHY

Every time I drive by the head of Loch Awe and pass the ruins of Kilchurn Castle, I see the turn-off for the old township of Stronmilchan, and I always find myself thinking about the dogs that gave the place its name.

Sròn nam Mialchoin – the promontory or point of the coursing hounds. A name carved into the land itself. It speaks of a time when deerhounds loped through these hills, swift and sure-footed, capable of catching a hare with grace or bringing down a stag with strength. These weren't pets; they were hunting partners, honoured enough to leave their name in places that mattered to the people.

And it's not the only place: you'll find names like these all over the Highlands, such as Coire nan Con, the corrie of the dogs, high above Glen Affric. Allt a' Mhadaidh, the stream of the dog, flowing down from the Black Cuillin peak Sgùrr a' Mhadaidh in the Isle of Skye. Loch nam Madadh, the loch of the hounds, now known to many as Lochmaddy,

where the Skye ferry from Uig arrives in North Uist. Caisteal nan Con, the castle of the hounds, a tumble of stones in Killundine, Morvern. Oral tradition links it to Aros Castle in Mull, just across the water, perhaps once a hunting lodge of the Lords of the Isles.

These canine co-ordinates are small reminders, scattered across the map, that dogs were part of the work, part of the hunt, and integral to the story of the terrain. Even now, when you hear those names, it's not hard to picture a shadowy, rough-coated shape swiftly moving across the hillside. Revered by chieftains and coveted by kings, the deerhound has earned its title as the Royal Dog of Scotland.

HIGHLAND HOUND OF LEGEND

Scottish deerhounds look like something out of a Highland fairytale: tall, shaggy and unexpectedly chic. In contrast to the Irish wolfhound – heavier set and chunkier in build – the deerhound is lighter on its feet, more refined in outline, sleeker in form. Their spirit runs deep in Scottish folklore: the Cù-Sìth, a spectral hound, was said to roam the moors as an omen of death. It's described in Gaelic legend as an otherworldly dog "as large as a small cow" hunting in eerie silence. Only its ghostly three barks would betray its presence – and woe betide the traveller who hadn't reached safety by the third.

Such tales of spectres in the form of great hounds have been passed through generations to haunt Highland imaginations. Described in oral traditions and collected in nineteenth-century folklore accounts, these stories blur the lines between the real and the otherworldly. Clan legends, too, spoke of phantom deerhounds – the Grey Dog of Meoble, An Cù Ghlas Mheòbhail, was a deerhound that would appear when a member of Clan MacDonald in Morar was about to die.

Equally, deerhounds pad their way through the stories of mythical heroes. According to legend, the warrior Fionn MacCumhaill, known by Scottish people as Fingal, had two majestic hounds, Bran and Sgeòlan, who were said to be his own kin transformed by enchantment.

These stories, known in Scotland as the Fingalian sagas – and to our Celtic cousins in Ireland as the Fenian Cycle – were passed down through our shared Gaelic oral tradition.

In later Ossianic praise poetry, these hounds are celebrated in words that epitomise a deerhound's form:

> *An eye of sloe with ear not low,*
> *With horse's breast, with depth of chest,*
> *With breadth of loin and curve in groin,*
> *And nape set far behind the head –*
> *Such were the dogs that Fingal bred.*

On the outskirts of bonnie Oban, below the cliffs of Dunollie Castle, a solitary giant boulder stands proud. Clach a' Choin – the Dog Stone – is said to be where Fingal would tether his favourite of the two dogs, Bran. Around the base of the rock is a groove worn by the chained pacing of the great hound as he waited for his master to return from crusade.

So esteemed was a mialchù – a dog of the highest order – that gaining a hound's loyalty was considered the utmost honour. The Irish hero Cú Chulainn earned his name – "the Hound of Culann" – after he killed a great dog and offered to take its place. It's a tale that echoes through Celtic storytelling, where the bond between hunter and hound is not only close, but sacred.

IF THE STONES COULD BARK

The Pictish stones of the Dark Ages show carved scenes of deer being pursued by slender, long-tailed dogs. On the Hilton of Cadboll Stone – an eighth-century slab from Easter Ross now on display in the National Museum of Scotland, Edinburgh – formidable hounds stretch out in full stride beneath their mounted hunters, running down a stag. The Eassie Stone from Angus (late 600s) likewise shows a hunter on foot with a spear, accompanied by a hound chasing a stag. This portrait is remarkably lifelike, down to the stag's muscled form and the determined stance of the dog.

Centuries later, at St Clement's Church in Rodel, Harris, a place of deep significance to Clan MacLeod, another scene is carved in stone. The ornate tomb of Alasdair Crotach MacLeod, the eighth chief, built in 1528, offers a rich insight into the world of a Highland leader. Alongside scenes of biblical devotion are elaborate carvings of proud birlinns, their oars arrayed in rhythm, symbols of seafaring strength and clan identity. Alongside them, a vivid hunting frieze unfolds, with mounted warriors carrying spears and deerhounds in full stride, racing down a stag. These are no idle decorations, but a record of sovereignty, honour and life lived in the Gaelic tradition, where horse and hound ran always at the chief's side.

THE HIGHLAND HUNTER

Long before the invention of firearms, when stags were hunted on foot with spear and sword, the Scottish deerhound was bred to bring them down.

Used by Highland chiefs and noblemen as early as the sixteenth century, and probably long before, the breed was designed for stamina, speed and strength. A single deerhound could pursue, overtake and wrestle a fully grown red deer to the ground – a feat demanding immense power, precise timing and unbreakable nerve.

Their role was not merely utilitarian. Deerhounds were prized by the nobility, and at times in Scottish history, only those of earl rank or above could own one. For those of lower standing, a leth-chù – a lurcher – might be gifted as a reward, a present capable of bringing home dinner in the form of a hare.

A BREED ON THE BRINK

By the late eighteenth century, only a few lines remained, and these were preserved largely by chance and passion. Among the most influential figures in the breed's survival were Archibald and Duncan McNeill, the latter becoming Lord Colonsay.

In the 1820s, the McNeill brothers undertook a dedicated programme to revive the Scottish deerhound. Drawing from a dwindling pool of dogs, they bred carefully to restore the breed's strength, type and character. "Should they once be lost," Archibald wrote, "it is difficult to imagine how any race of dogs can again be produced possessing such a combination of qualities." Their commitment to preserving both form and function laid a foundation that modern breeders still build upon. In fact, every deerhound alive today can trace its lineage back to those few hounds the McNeills saved.

Their efforts came at a time when the breed's extinction seemed inevitable. Thanks to their understanding of its history and physical needs, the deerhound survived long enough to win new admirers, including Queen Victoria and Prince Albert. A painting from around 1838 by Sir Edwin Landseer, held in the Royal Collection, depicts some of the queen's favourite pets: Hector the deerhound, Nero the greyhound, Dash the spaniel and a parrot named Lory.

The two world wars were especially hard on short-lived, estate-based breeds like the deerhound; with landholdings fractured and the sporting life in retreat, the breed again came close to disappearing. Only the quiet commitment of a few keepers kept it going – notably Miss Marjorie Bell, who was a steady presence in her world of Enterkine hounds.

Anastasia Noble, over seven decades, shaped the Ardkinglas line from a single female, Nora of Enterkine, gifted to her as a pet from Miss Bell. She went on to oversee 135 litters, twenty-four champions and exports worldwide, bringing joy to the hunt, the show ring and all who shared her passion. Their friendship again maintained the steady heartbeat of a tradition, as ever it is for those people who toil on behalf of endangered breeds.

Today's deerhound owners, too, are more than companions: they are the stewards of the breed, carrying forward a legacy shaped by centuries – yet the future of the Scottish deerhound depends not on fame or fashion, but on people who care. Breed clubs are ready to welcome new hands, so whether you're curious, committed or simply considering – get in touch.

If the deerhound has stirred something in you, don't wait. Reach out, meet dogs in real life, learn more. Be part of the story! These amazing hounds have stood by us through legend and now it's our turn to stand by them.

ANNE & THE HUMBIEHOUNDS

In Humbie, East Lothian – a village so peaceful that even the cockerel thinks twice before crowing – Anne shares her home with a trio of Scottish deerhounds and one irrepressible wee terrier. The deerhounds are gracefully, gloriously shaggy. The terrier is small, determined – and allegedly in charge. Anne grew up in Edinburgh but has lived in Humbie for over twenty-five years. She's had dogs all her life – rescues, lurchers, greyhounds, working terriers – but it was a deerhound-cross in her younger years that started it all. "There was just something about the stillness in him," she says. "A kind of knowing. Once a deerhound has found you, that's it."

The queen of the household is Laika – officially Gentiehun Iso Harmaa Koira at Humbiehounds – five years old, fiercely elegant and the mother of the pack. Her name, chosen by Anne's granddaughter in Finland, means "Big Grey Dog". "She thought all dogs were meant to look like deerhounds," Anne laughs. "Everything else was some other sort of animal entirely."

Laika came to Anne as a twelve-week-old pup, one of a litter of nine. When Anne arrived to meet them, the pups were let out into the garden en masse – a flurry of limbs, fluff and curiosity. But one small dark shape padded over, sat down next to her and didn't budge. "She chose me," Anne says. "I didn't really have a say."

As a show dog, Laika's heart was never quite in it. At ringcraft, she was known as the "Dourhound", stoically enduring each go-round with the resigned look of someone at a damp bus stop. But let her off the lead in the fields and hills of East Lothian and she comes alive – galloping, splashing, nose to the wind. "She's never looked happier than up to her armpits in bog," says Anne. "And that's just fine by me."

When the time came to breed from her, Anne paired Laika with a grand old lad named Sleat. The result was six beautiful puppies named Torrin, Tam, Rita, Ivy, Flora and Beira. Each one found the person meant for them – or the other way around. Anne's friend Sheila, the owner of Sleat, sadly lost him just two weeks after the pups were born. She'd already committed to another puppy elsewhere, but when she laid eyes on puppy Torrin – the image of his dad – she couldn't walk away. "It's not easy taking on two pups at once," Anne admits, "but sometimes your heart makes the decision for you." And that's what happened for Sheila.

Today, many of Laika's pups are thriving in the show world, including Tam and Ivy. Flora, the angelic one, took to good manners suspiciously easily. Beira, meanwhile, remains the wild card ("mad as a hatter, but utterly adored"). Rita, the one who stayed, is Anne's "spirit animal" – fast, fierce and full of fire. "She's the turbo-charged version of a deerhound," Anne says. "Built for comfort and speed."

Laika was later mated to Hunter, resulting in a single pup, Layla. Anne jokes about how I took a shine to her when I was filming *Cù Leis Thu?* for BBC Alba. Then, as she likes to tell everyone, she caught me "trying to smuggle her out in his pocket". Layla stayed. She's the image of her mum, dark and sharp, and has done well in the show ring – though she'd rather be lolloping up a hill than standing still for a judge.

And then there's Koira – the wild card terrier with the hardscrabble soul of a scrapper and the bounce of a rubber ball. A Bichon cross Jack Russell mix, Koira arrived as a hand-reared rescue pup from Ireland. Anne wasn't planning on another dog, especially not a tiny one, but when her beloved old deerhound died, something shifted. "I needed a change," she says. "Something to shake up the grief." Koira arrived and promptly took charge of the entire household. "She's five kilos of chaos, but she's earned her place." A deerhound pack, it seems, should have a wee fighter of a boss dog at their dainty heels!

Anne has devoted her time to the deerhounds: breeding carefully, showing occasionally and always keeping the big picture in mind. "There are so few of them," she says. "The gene pool is tiny.

But they're worth saving. They get under your skin. Into your bones."

She stays in touch with all her pups and their owners, often from the litters she bred back in 2007. She's also involved in rescue work – home-checking, fostering and transporting. "If I can help a hound on its way, I will," she says. "It's what we do." But it's not just about the dogs. A pack like Anne's often draws a second pack around it – one made of people. And among Scottish deerhound owners, that human pack can be very closely bonded.

There's something about this breed – their deep need for companionship, their preference for their own kind (sighthounds recognise and like to get to know one another, while displaying an indifference bordering on disdain towards other breeds), their galloping joy when let loose together in a field – that naturally brings their humans into orbit with one another. Perhaps it's awareness of their sometimes shorter lives, which sharpens the sense of urgency. Or maybe it's their need for space, for expansive places to run free, which nudges their owners into cooperation and fellow feeling. Or maybe it's simply that unspoken calling of like to like. People who love deerhounds tend to be kindred spirits.

Whatever the reason, the result is a network of friendship, support and long-term desire to see the breed thrive, which creates a human pack as loyal and thoughtful as the dogs they cherish.

Anne is very much a part of that pack. Sheila, for instance, is the keeper of the two big lads called Torrin and Faolin, sons of Laika. Jean's lovely girl Arwen recently had her first litter with Torrin; six pups – three boys, three girls – all now happily homed. Jean first met Anne at a Christmas dog show, where Anne's first litter had gathered with their owners in festive jumpers and elf hats with the deerhounds in matching reindeer antlers and bells. For fun, the whole group did a lap of honour, a moment Jean remembers fondly: "It made me feel like part of a much bigger community."

Their friendship deepened when Anne offered to be her birthing partner for Arwen's litter. "She supported me throughout the pregnancy and was in constant touch during whelping and beyond. Her knowledge and support were invaluable." Anne's advice that new deerhound mums respond well to shortbread also turned out to be true, and Jean admits she quite enjoyed a wee piece herself. "It made me really appreciate what a supportive community there is among deerhound owners, with a selfless love of the breed." I'm pleased to report that Arwen's pups Merlin, Morar, Vaila, Ghillie and Roag are now all happily homed. (Thyra stayed with her mum and Jean!) The circle grew that wee bit wider, the deerhound community that wee bit stronger.

Oh, and as I write these words, Angie's beloved Katie Morag has just been mated with Torrin and early scans show she is expecting a larger than normal litter – another match made through careful timing, shared knowledge, genealogical understanding and deep mutual trust. *(Note to Coinneach: please can we get one when those pups are born?)*

These are rooted friendships, not casual connections. These remarkable women are custodians of these lines, and they are there for each other and in it together. With good folk like this at the helm, the future of the Scottish deerhound feels luminous with possibility.

And what of the breed itself? Anne sums it up: "They're loyal, but not needy. Independent, but affectionate. You don't own a deerhound – you belong to them. They're not just part of the family: they become part of the furniture, part of the landscape. You'll never be anonymous with one beside you. They're the kind of dog that stops traffic and starts conversations."

She pauses, then smiles. "If a deerhound chooses you, that's it. You're theirs. For life."

A TERRIER ON THE TRAIL

The Cairn Terrier

BREED STANDARD

GENERAL APPEARANCE: Alert, hardy and active. Dark points at ears and muzzle are very typical.
COAT: Harsh, weather-resistant outer coat with soft undercoat.
COLOUR: Cream, wheaten, red, grey, brindle or nearly black.
EYES: Dark hazel, set wide with bushy brows.
MOVEMENT: Free and vigorous with good reach and drive.
TEMPERAMENT: Independent, cheerful, courageous and intelligent.

A DOG SHAPED BY STONES

If you've ever scrambled across a Highland hillside and caught sight of a wiry wee terrier darting among the rocks as if it owned the place, chances are you've met a Cairn. Rough-coated, sharp-eyed and low to the ground, in all respects the Cairn terrier is a true product of Scotland's gloriously wild landscapes. The word *terrier* comes from the Latin *terra*, meaning earth, and these were truly earth dogs – bred to dig, bolt, chase and defend.

Renowned as a scruffy, stubborn, delightful wee toerag, the Cairn earned its place the hard way, amid stones and heather. A working dog first and foremost, it could be found clearing foxes from crofts, rats from barns and otters from burns. The land forged the dog, and in turn the dog kept the land clear. Unlike some of its fancier relations, the Cairn stayed close to its roots – it was bred to think as well as chase, to puzzle out where the crafty fox had gone, or root out a cunning stoat from a hiding place.

The Cairn is small enough to slip between rocks, hardy enough to shrug off spiky thorns and brutal weather. It's watchful enough to spot a flicker of movement on the hillside. A tough worker who's cheeky enough to land top spot on your knee. As you can well imagine, they don't ask for permission to be part of your life, but simply strut in and stake a claim.

Their head is strong, with a broad skull and keen, dark hazel eyes peeking out from beneath shaggy brows. Ears are small, sharp-pointed and erect, giving them an alert, inquisitive look. A Cairn moves freely and boldly – their feet are strong with thick pads and forefeet slightly larger than the hinds, mainly for grip.

The coat is dense and harsh, the tail is short and carried with cheer, and according to the Kennel Club's standard, the Cairn must give a general foxy appearance. That doesn't mean slyness – it means they are quick and sharp with a bright, intelligent face. They are extremely loveable and alert, with an effortlessly brisk, workmanlike appearance.

THE CAIRN AT HOME

If you bring a Cairn into your home, you'll find yourself sharing your days with a companion who is busy, clever and endlessly entertaining. They're naturally curious, keen to inspect every corner of the house before heading out to patrol the garden after real or imagined intruders. Indoors, they're affectionate without being clingy. They might be happiest at your side, but are also quite content to make their own plans if you're otherwise occupied.

GROUP: Terrier.
STATUS: Stable, but low, with signs of gradual decline.
ORIGIN: The Cairn is widely thought of as the progenitor of the West Coast terrier group, and was bred to tackle vermin and guard small holdings.
HEIGHT: 28–31 cm.
WEIGHT: 6.5–7 kg.

Socialisation
Friendliness
Trainability

Size

Colour

Cairns are great all-rounders; they're always up for country walks, yet their small stature means they're happy to live with you in a town flat. They're alert little watchdogs, barking a brief warning when something's amiss, but they're generally not too yappy. Training a Cairn takes a sense of humour – they're smart and strong-willed. These wee tykes like to know why they are doing something, a leftover from generations of independent working terriers who could think and improvise. Positive training, variety and plenty of games will work wonders. Be careful, though: any tension will only breed stubbornness in your terrier.

Cairns form strong bonds with their families, but they won't glue themselves to you like a lapdog. Certainly, they will anchor themselves to your daily life: trotting along as you move about your day, supervising your tasks with that foxy interest of theirs. Once they trust you, their loyalty runs deep, steady as bedrock.

Grooming is simple – regular brushing, the occasional bath and some hand-stripping to keep that coat in top working condition. No elaborate cuts, no fancy trims: a Cairn should always look like it's ready to head up the glen. Generally a healthy breed, Cairns will eat what they're given, sleep where they please and often live well into their teens – their feisty terrier spirit carries them a long way. I like to think of them as the dog form of my favourite plumber, turning up in blue overalls, fixing whatever's broken without batting an eyelid, sipping a mug of builder's tea, and having a blether while they work. Dependable, practical and full of good cheer, that's the Cairn terrier to a tee.

ROUGH ORIGINS & ROCKY HISTORY

Before there were Westies or Scotties or show-bred Skyes, there were simply Scottish terriers: rough-coated, game little dogs used by crofters, ghillies and farmers from the Borders to the

Hebrides. The Cairn's story is rooted and tangled in these early dogs which formed the base of the wee workers we know now.

In the nineteenth century, selective breeding started to tease the types apart; some were smoother-coated, some longer-backed, some lower slung. But in the western Highlands and islands, a particularly hardy kind of terrier remained – small, shaggy, sharp as a tack. These were the dogs we now call Cairns.

Their name comes straight from their work. A cairn – from Gaelic càrn – is a pile of stones, often marking a boundary or a burial site. Vermin loved them for their hiding places, which meant that crofters needed a dog nimble enough to wriggle inside and brave enough to flush them out – and so the Cairn was shaped.

There's good evidence they developed most strongly around mainland Argyllshire, the Isle of Mull and towards Skye – the rougher the ground, the tougher the terrier. It is said that during his reign King James VI of Scotland sent six "earthe dogges" from Argyll to the King of France, prized gifts from a country that knew the worth of a working terrier.

But it wasn't until 1912 that the Kennel Club officially recognised the breed as the Cairn terrier, setting it apart from its close cousins. Before that, they might be labelled short-coated Skyes or

> **DID YOU KNOW?**
> **BITE-SIZED CAIRN**
> - **Digging Dynamos:** Cairns' front paws are larger than their rear ones, equipping them perfectly for digging into rocky crevices in pursuit of prey.
> - **The Cairn's Vocal Signature:** These terriers are known for their distinctive bark; they are often described as having a unique "burr".
> - **Royal Cargo:** King James VI of Scotland (later James I of England) esteemed Scottish earth dogs so highly that he sent them as gifts to European monarchs. To safeguard these prized canines during sea voyages, he ensured they travelled on separate ships to prevent the loss of the entire group in case of disaster.
> - **The Short-Haired Skye:** Before being recognised as a distinct breed, Cairn terriers were often referred to as short-haired Skye terriers in early shows. This continued until 1912 when the Kennel Club formally acknowledged the Cairn.

simply cairn dogs. Today, the Cairn is still considered one of the closest living links to Scotland's original earth dogs.

A CLAN OF CHARACTERS

One woman in particular played a vital role in bringing the Cairn into public recognition. Ida Monro was born in 1871 in Palamcottah, India, where her father served as a captain in the British army. Returning to Scotland during her childhood, her family settled in Edinburgh, where her father rose to become Inspector of Constabulary for Scotland, receiving a knighthood in 1894. However, it was from her mother – who had acquired dogs from Skye in the 1870s – that Ida inherited her passion for the rugged terriers of the Highlands. This passion never left her, and Ida continued to dedicate herself to preserving and promoting Scotland's native breeds for the rest of her life.

In 1893, she married Major Alastair Campbell of the Seaforth Highlanders, and upon his retirement in 1903, the couple established their home in Ardrishaig, Argyllshire. In 1909, Ida – who by now had fallen in love with the Cairns – exhibited her dogs at the Inverness Show under the breed name Prick-Eared Skyes. This move sparked controversy among Skye terrier enthusiasts, leading to debates in the dog press.

Ida's dedication to the breed was unwavering. After the Kennel Club formally accepted the Cairn terrier as a breed, she became the first Honorary Secretary of the newly formed Cairn Terrier Club, helping to shape and safeguard its future. She then developed the renowned Brocaire line, producing champions like Gesto, MacLeod of MacLeod, Doran Bhan, Roy Mhor and Calla Mhor – dogs that helped define the breed's early standard in both appearance and temperament.

Association with royalty further bolstered the Cairn terrier's popularity, with Baroness Burton, a prominent breeder and owner of the Dochfour Kennels near Inverness, playing a pivotal role. The Baroness supplied several Cairns to the then Prince of Wales, later briefly King Edward VIII, including a foxy-faced little dog named Dochfour Molly. She attracted widespread attention when photographed alongside the Prince and Mrs Simpson, lending the breed a subtle but powerful royal endorsement.

Ida attended her last show – the championship show of the Cairn Terrier Club – just a short time before she died in 1946. However, it wasn't until 2000 that, in recognition of her contributions, the Cairn Terrier Club erected a plaque in her honour at the Royal School of Veterinary Studies in Edinburgh. The

> **DID YOU KNOW?**
> **BITE-SIZED CAIRN**
> - **Toto's Big Break:** The iconic role of Toto in the 1939 film *The Wizard of Oz* was played by a female Cairn terrier named Terry. She earned a weekly salary of $125 – the equivalent of over $2,600 today – a substantial sum that surpassed the earnings of many human actors on set.
> - **Chameleon Coats:** Cairn terrier puppies often undergo a fascinating transformation in coat colour as they mature. A pup born with a dark brindle coat might lighten to a sandy hue over time, making each Cairn a delightful "nature's surprise" package.
> - **The Hardiest of the Hard:** Cairn terriers are celebrated for their robust health and longevity. Many live well into their teens, maintaining their playful and energetic demeanour throughout their lives.

inscription reads, "In memory of Mrs. J. Alastair Campbell 1871–1946, who brought the Cairn Terrier out of obscurity and gave the world its best little pal."

DRAWING A WHITE LINE

People often confuse the Cairn terrier and the West Highland white terrier, and it's easy to see why. These canine cousins share common ancestry and were once part of the same rough-coated Highland terrier sub-family. Well into the nineteenth century, they likely interbred freely, and it wasn't unusual for puppies of varying coat colours – some wheaten, some brindle, some white – to appear in the same litter.

But as the art of dog shows gained popularity and breed clubs emerged in the late Victorian and Edwardian periods, formal distinctions were drawn. The white-coated pups began to be favoured by a group of fanciers who championed them as a separate type – a story I will delve into in the Westie chapter (see page 67). Eventually, the breeds were officially divided and, in 1924, the West Highland white terrier and the Cairn terrier were recognised as distinct breeds, and interbreeding between them was prohibited in 1925.

From that point on, the Cairn retained its rugged, earthy palette – wheaten, red, grey, cream, near black or brindling in all these tones. Never solid black, nor black and tan, and never ever pure white. That snowy hallmark became exclusive to the Westie: a proud declaration of difference that has endured ever since.

Today, whether trotting along a city pavement or racing across a Highland trail, a Cairn is still what it always was: a small dog with a great big heart. It doesn't need pampering or a fancy wee jacket; it just needs purpose, companionship and some room to roam. And if you ever find your garden newly excavated, or the insoles mysteriously removed from your shoes never to be found again, don't be too quick to scold. You're living with a Cairn – a dog born to move stones.

A CAIRN FOR THE HEART

Heather's heart had belonged to Ruby the Westie, who was full of spark from the start – an adventurous pup who quickly took charge of the household. They were inseparable. When Ruby sadly died in a road accident, the grief was profound. "She was my first dog, my shadow, my little boss," says Heather.

Friends could see that Heather needed a new pup in her life and they gently suggested she consider a Cairn terrier. Heather, still heartsore, wasn't sure. "Everyone knows Toto, but I'd never actually met a Cairn," Heather admits, but that soon changed at the Cairn Terrier Club annual Championship Show, which was happening in Penicuik, near Edinburgh, the following weekend.

"I dragged my mum and partner along – it was Mother's Day and none of us had ever been to a dog show before!" Something clicked for Heather as she admired the dogs: their range of colours, their confidence and their character. "We didn't know it at the time," she chuckles, "but we were watching our future breeder in the ring."

A few weeks later, the club put her in touch with a litter in Doncaster, and Heather welcomed a new pup – a wee brindle whirlwind with the Sunday name of Furythor Orion, but whom she named Harris, after her favourite gin.

That summer, they visited the Isle of Harris together. "It felt like the name was meant to be."

Harris, now three, is true to his breed. Independent, clever and full of personality, he prefers the company of other dogs on walks but never strays far from home comforts. At night, he's not on the sofa, but close by – stretched out on the floor or cooried into his den under the hallway cabinet. He's fearless with most things, except water, and has a strong sense of routine. "He knows when I need to finish work and take him out," says Heather. "He's my reminder to step away from the laptop."

Training, however, was no small task. "I'd forgotten just how intense puppies can be," Heather sighs with a smile. "A few days in, I was sitting on the floor in the early morning thinking, What have I done?" But with focus, games and firm boundaries, things began to settle. "Once the puppy teeth were gone, I never looked back."

Heather threw herself into the world of Cairns – joining walking groups, attending breed fun days and eventually becoming treasurer of the Cairn Terrier Club. She even learned to hand-strip Harris's coat, taking grooming at his pace, not hers. "He's taught me patience like no other dog."

To help promote the breed, she decided to try showing. "It's not something I'd ever imagined. I was the complete novice. He had champions in his pedigree, but I had no clue what I was doing!" But it became a way to meet other Cairn lovers and share their enthusiasm for a breed whose numbers have declined since their heyday in the mid-twentieth century.

Cairns are endlessly rewarding, and Harris is playful, affectionate in his own way, and always up for an adventure – or a good potter round the garden, keeping a keen eye on things. "He's my loveable, excitable, independent companion," says Heather. "As happy climbing hills as he is watching the world go by."

THE GHILLIE WITH A SCHOTTISCHE-LIKE SWAGGER

In the village of Longside, in northeast Scotland, lives a small dog with a big bark and even bigger opinions. Ghillie is a two-year-old Cairn terrier with a scruffy coat, a proud strut and the kind of personality that fills a room with cèilidh energy before he's even waltzed through the door.

His pedigree name is Cornton Summer Special – born on Midsummer's Day, he was the surprise third pup in his litter, arriving a full day after his siblings! The breeder joked that "Some / Are / Special", and Ghillie's been proving it ever since.

The name suits him twice over. In Gaelic, gille means a young lad or loyal attendant – a perfect fit for a dog who shadows his people with fierce devotion and wild enthusiasm, whether hiking the hills or gatecrashing an online business meeting. At home, he's affectionate, but never needily so. He prances like a show pony, steals socks like he's paid to do it, and greets Milly home from work with full-throated howls and a vertical leap that would make a collie jealous.

Milly grew up with Labradors, but it was her husband, Scott, who introduced her to Cairns – himself inspired by happy memories of a childhood friendship with a little black terrier called Sooty. Their first dog together was Maggie, a Cairn with fifteen years of love under her collar. After she passed, Milly contacted Maggie's breeder and, through the wonderful world of Cairn terrier connections, was offered a pup from two of Scotland's most respected lines: Cornton and Birselaw. Ghillie came from the final Cornton litter, and with the Birselaw breeder now sadly gone, he is among the last of his type. A pedigree within a pedigree, Scott and Milly agreed to let him sire a litter to help preserve the lines.

That decision was the beginning of something unexpected. Milly looked up the Cairn Terrier Club of Scotland and discovered a championship show just three weeks away. "Folk train for years," she laughs. "We had twenty-one days and no clue."

Ghillie, naturally, took it all in his stride. Since then, he's earned rosettes, sired a litter of four and grown into the kind of dog who belongs in the spotlight. Milly's even got her eye on Crufts 2026. "Just to say we've been," she admits with a beaming smile. One to watch, this lad could turn a few heads on that famous green carpet.

Milly is now a proud club member and fierce supporter of Scotland's native breeds. "We were shocked when we learned Cairns had recently been on the 'at watch' list," she says. "How can a dog so Scottish, so full of grit and charm, be in danger of disappearing?"

But Ghillie's charm isn't present only in the ring. He's a hoover-fighter (just ask the gaffer-taped hose), a leaf-chaser and an under-bed-crawling outlaw. His coat – scruffy as a thatched roof in a gale, sometimes backcombed to punkish effect by the elements – is part of his rugged Highland appeal. He's happiest when filthy, refuses to wear a jacket in the snow and howls mournfully if he catches a lady dog's scent on his way home from the park. Miles of heartbreak – every time!

Ghillie is also stunningly clever. Puzzle toys don't last long, and he knows exactly how to get his own way on a walk – usually by ignoring instructions until bribed. But these, of course, are the very traits that make us love terriers! He's quick on his feet, strong in his convictions and likes to dictate the route.

Scott lives with some health issues, and Ghillie has an unusual, uncanny instinct for care. If Scott slows, Ghillie stops. He stares up at him, silent and watchful, as if asking, *You all right, boss?* On difficult days, he brings joy. On easy days, he brings a healthy modicum of chaos. On all days, he brings love.

"He's the best wee pal in the world," says Milly, echoing the very words of the plaque dedicated to the indomitable Ida Monro. "Our life revolves around Ghillie – and we wouldn't have it any other way."

HEART
OF THE
HEBRIDES

The Skye Terrier

BREED STANDARD

GENERAL APPEARANCE: Long, low, and elegant, with a level topline and strong bone structure.
COAT: Straight, hard, flat topcoat with a short, soft undercoat. Falls gracefully to each side of a natural parting along the back.
COLOUR: Black, dark or light grey, cream, or fawn – all with black points (ears, muzzle and tail tip).
EYES: Brown, medium-sized, close-set, with a soft, intelligent expression.
EARS: Prick or drop.
MOVEMENT: Free and active, with a seemingly effortless gait despite the low frame.
TEMPERAMENT: A "one person" dog. Reserved with strangers, dignified, courageous and discerning. Never vicious.

SKYE'S LOYAL LITTLE LEGEND

Legends loom large in the Scottish islands, and this terrier is as much a part of the island's dualchas or heritage as the Gaelic language, the Cuillin hills, Dunvegan Castle or the bridge that now ties it to the mainland. Through all its journeys, the Skye terrier has stayed true to its roots – a distinctly Gàidhealach dog with a loyal demeanour, a sharp mind and a spirit shaped by its Hebridean home. Luckily for visitors to the island, despite their rarity, there are still a few Skyes to be spotted around the villages of Eilean a' Cheò – and where better to spy one than in the natural environment of its original home?

TEMPERAMENT – DEVOTED, DIGNIFIED & FEARLESS

Spend a bit of time with a Skye terrier and one word inevitably comes to mind – loyal. This breed forms a bond with its family that is deep and unshakable. A Skye might choose one special person – their favourite human – and become their shadow, but that doesn't mean they lack affection towards other people in their orbit. They can be playful and will show a funny, warm side when they are in their comfort zone. Don't be surprised to find your Skye snuggled beside you on the sofa, long tail gently thumping whenever you glance their way: they live for companionship and closeness.

That said, Skye terriers carry themselves with a certain dignified reserve – they simply aren't the all-round, full-on extroverts that some other terriers like to be. Strangers will earn a polite sniff, perhaps a wary eye – but probably not instant friendship; that has to be earned in time. Early socialisation can help them warm to new people, but at heart these dogs are discerning, independent and can be somewhat aloof. They choose friends carefully. I, for one, think these are admirable traits, setting them apart from their terrier cousins.

One of the Skye terrier's most distinctive features is its ears – some have prick ears, standing upright and alert beneath the fall of hair, and others have drop ears, folding neatly down to frame the face. In the early days of the show ring, drop-eared Skyes were often preferred. Queen Victoria's own Skye terriers were said to have had drop ears. However, as time went on, prick-eared Skyes – with their proud stance – grew in popularity too, especially among breeders who admired the alert expression it gave the dogs. Today, both ear types are equally accepted under the breed standard, and neither is considered more correct than the other – it's simply a matter of individual preference.

GROUP: Terrier.
STATUS: Vulnerable.
ORIGIN: From the Isle of Skye, a distinct, long, low and hardy terrier that was bred to hunt foxes, badgers and otters among rocky terrain. Legend suggests they may even have Viking ancestry.
HEIGHT: 25–26 cm at the shoulder.
WEIGHT: Male: 16–18 kg. Female: 11–14 kg.

Socialisation
Friendliness
Trainability

Size

Colour

LOOKING AFTER YOUR SKYE TERRIER

The Skye's flowing coat is one of its most striking features. It parts down the middle of the back and cascades towards the ground like a fringed shawl – beautiful, yes, but also fairly high-maintenance. Regular brushing two to three times a week is a must to prevent tangles and mats – a pin brush or fine comb will become your best pal. Pay extra attention to the feathering on the ears, legs and belly. These terriers have a way of collecting the great outdoors in their coat after every walk. Leaves, twigs, burrs and briars all love to hitch a ride in that long hair!

True to their working roots, Skye terriers enjoy activity, but they are not as hyper as some other dogs. A solid hour of exercise a day – brisk walks, playtime in the garden or interactive games – will keep them in good spirits. They love to sniff and explore, and their nose will happily lead them along hedgerows, gullies and hiking trails, but they are more a glen dweller than a mountaineer – so probably not a dog to scale the Black Cuillins with you. Once they've had their exercise, they are actually quite content to have a norrag in a sunny spot on the carpet, paws crossed and dozing in the warmth.

While a Skye is small enough for an urban life in a flat, remember that they are a bit longer and heavier than your average lapdog. A Skye will appreciate having some room to stretch out and, be warned, they quite like having a sofa to call their own. Also consider any stairs in your home – those wee legs work hard on steps, and frequent climbing may strain a long back.

Skye terriers can be vocal. They will let you know if someone's at the door, if the postie is two houses down or if a squirrel dares to intrude on *their* lawn. This makes them superb little watchdogs – they take the job seriously – but in a town setting, the constant alerts

might need management. Training them to a cue like "sguir dheth" or "enough", or redirecting the barking into a game can help. However, you'll never entirely silence a Skye's protective instinct, and truth be told, you wouldn't want to. That alertness is part of their charm.

You will become something of an ambassador when you own a Skye terrier. People will stop you in the street to ask, "What kind of dog *is that?*" and likely be tickled by the answer. Be prepared for admirers. After all, it's not every day one sees a little dog that looks like a walking shaggy ottoman with such natural poise! Belonging to a Skye is a joy, but also a responsibility to showcase the breed's best qualities so that this Scottish treasure wins more hearts. (Given their rarity and specialness, that goes for all our Scottish native breeds.)

ORIGINS WREATHED IN BOG MYRTLE & MYTH

Like many old Scottish breeds, the exact origins of the Skye terrier blend folklore with fact. Some say the story begins in 1588 with shipwrecks from the Spanish Armada when, according to legend, several small, long-coated canines – perhaps Maltese-like dogs – swam ashore after galleons sank off Skye's rocky coast. These exotic survivors, so the tale goes, found their way into local terrier stock and lent a

---

DID YOU KNOW? BITE-SIZED SKYE

- **Greyfriars Bobby:** Perhaps one of the most famous dogs in the world, Bobby was widely believed to be a Skye terrier. In 1873, the year after he died, a public subscription raised money to erect a bronze statue in his honour – now one of Edinburgh's best-loved landmarks.
- **Queen's Little Companions:** Tradition holds that Mary, Queen of Scots is said to have brought one of her beloved Skye terriers with her to the executioner's block in 1587, hiding the small dog in her skirts until the final moment.
- **Dougal the TV Star:** The shaggy, endearing Dougal from *The Magic Roundabout* was modelled on a drop-eared Skye terrier. Creator Serge Danot gave him a world-weary yet loveable personality, very much in keeping with a Skye.

dash of silken glamour to the island dogs. Whether or not this particular tale is true, it has added a fitting air of romance to the Skye's windswept beginnings.

What we do know is that by the sixteenth century, small sturdy terriers were thriving in Skye and the nearby Highlands. These dogs weren't pampered pets: they were hardy working terriers, fearless exterminators (or at least deterrents) of foxes, badgers and otters that were considered a pest by those who worked the land. Short legs and a long body gave them an agility boost underground, while a thick, flowing coat protected against brambles and biting vermin. One early description praised the Skye terrier as a dog that would "*fearlessly go to ground against any foe*", emerging tousled but triumphant.

Even among the great houses of Skye, the terriers earned their place. Clan Donald, whose ancestral seat lay at Armadale on the Sleat peninsula, is said to have kept a distinguished line of long-coated dogs during the eighteenth and early nineteenth centuries. Lady MacDonald herself reportedly maintained a kennel of elegant terriers, lending distinguished early favour and refinement

to the breed. Although Armadale Castle was not completed until 1815, the clan's presence – and its traditions – in Skye stretch back centuries. The link between Skye terriers and the grand Highland houses helped shape the breed's early story, long before dog shows and Victorian fashion made them famous.

Terriers formed an important part of the agrarian systems of land management, which were part of everyday Highland life, making these dogs implicitly trusted for their grit and gusto. Crofters and ghillies bred them out of pragmatic need, but it was often those living in the sphere of the grand houses who began to take an interest in shaping bloodlines. In an age where *improvement* – in cattle, horses and dogs alike – was à la mode, selective breeding became both a hobby and a marker of discernment. To cultivate a finer type of dog was to demonstrate good taste and knowledge, and over time the rough working terriers were honed into distinct breeds. Their natural toughness softened just enough to catch the eye of the lords and ladies, and gradually they made their way into the parlours – and no doubt onto the chaise longues – of the big houses.

In Skye, the Waternish terriers stood out as some of the best – hardy, game little dogs that could work sea-cliffs and moorland with equal ease. Major Allan MacDonald of Waternish kept his working pack and helped bring the breed into wider recognition. His family's dogs not only shaped the Skye terrier we know today, but even found their way halfway around the world, laying the foundations of the Australian terrier.

FROM CROFTS TO CASTLES

The coming of the railways in the mid-nineteenth century changed everything in the Scottish Highlands. For the first time, visitors from the south could reach these previously inaccessible areas with relative ease, drawn north by the lure of wild beauty and

> **DID YOU KNOW?**
> **BITE-SIZED SKYE**
> - **Twice as Long as Tall:** A Skye should be twice as long as he is tall at the shoulder. This distinct outline comes from a form of dwarfism shared with the dachshund and corgi.
> - **A Clause in Parliament:** In the late 1800s, Skye terriers were so popular they were specifically mentioned in debates over the Cruelty to Animals Act due to rising theft of fashionable dogs.
> - **Whispers of Viking Dogs:** Some believe the Skye terrier carries echoes of Viking dogs – low and long hounds like the Swedish Vallhund or Drever, brought ashore by early Norse settlers.

romantic landscapes. Soon, travellers to the Highlands began to take note of these distinctive terriers, and fanciers from the south were quickly enchanted. In 1842, none other than Queen Victoria acquired a Skye terrier – and she soon grew fond not just of the breed, but of Scotland itself. Her purchase of Balmoral Castle ten years later helped catapult Scottish identity into the wider cultural spotlight, and with it, the Skye terrier.

Royal favour landed the Skye at the height of fashion and these rough-coated hunters found themselves lifted from farmyard to finery. Victorian ladies fell in love with the Skye's elegant looks and loyal heart, and by the 1860s, it was said a proper duchess "would be ashamed to be seen in the park without her Skye terrier at the leash".

Artists, too, immortalised the breed's charm, Sir Edwin Landseer, famed painter of animals, produced affectionate portraits of Skye terriers reclining on velvet cushions, and their flowing coats and soulful eyes in high society settings served only to increase their appeal and canine cachet. Chromolithographs of Skye terriers appeared in the pages of Vero Shaw's *Illustrated Book of the Dog* in 1881, showing the world the Skye's distinctive form. What had been a humble hill dog was now an icon of the Victorian upper classes.

GREYFRIARS BOBBY – A TERRIER'S TALE

Perhaps the most enduring story of loyalty was the tale of Greyfriars Bobby, traditionally thought to have been a Skye terrier. In 1850s Edinburgh, John Gray, a night watchman for the police, patrolled the dark, cobbled streets with his little dog by his side. The two were inseparable, keeping watch together through all weathers, but when Gray took ill and died in 1858, Bobby stoically refused to leave his master's graveside in Greyfriars Kirkyard.

Through bitter winters and drenching Scottish rains, Bobby kept his vigil – for fourteen long years – as his story warmed hearts across the city. Locals brought him food and even built him a shelter beside the grave. When Bobby himself passed away in 1872, Edinburgh honoured him with a statue and an epitaph celebrating this terrier's "faithful devotion". To this day, visitors in their droves visit the statue of this wee Scottish dog – his nose worn to a golden hue from the hands of all those who pet him – who proved that canine loyalty knows no bounds.

A proud islander, true to its roots, in a world full of bigger, flashier breeds, these dogs stand out. And as long as there are cosy firesides and loving families to welcome them, their legend will continue, over the sea to Skye and beyond.

MARI & THE SKYE PACK

In Caithness, the wind doesn't blow, it rearranges your day. But no one wears a blustery forecast better than a Skye terrier, their coats billowing like flags of headstrong, capable independence. On a croft where the back door is always open and breakfast toast is shared at ten sharp, you'll find Mari and her four faithful companions: low-slung, long-fringed Skye terriers, affectionately nicknamed the Bendy Bus Brigade. Two came from Bhatarnais lines, and two were born under Mari's own Headscrook affix – but at home, like all the best dogs, they each answer to toast.

Mari was born in her granny's stone cottage by Broken Cross Muir, and grew up travelling the Highlands in her dad's Volvo – back when the Rest and Be Thankful was still a single track with passing places. Her dad ran a civil engineering firm with a remit to upgrade roads, and Mari went with him from site to site, supervising jobs and liaising with clerks of works. Her first dog was a Westie called Sally, which was officially licensed as Sally Hamilton after five-year-old Mari insisted on giving her the family surname to the clerk at the post office counter.

Dogs have been part of the story ever

since – mostly rescues, always characters and never dull – but when retirement brought a stillness to the house, Mari declared, "Skye terrier. That's the dog for me." And she didn't start with one, but two.

At the home of Davina Matthews – a respected breeder from the Isle of Skye – Mari sat cross-legged on the floor and asked the tangle of puppies, "Well then, who wants to be Wyvis?" She'd already chosen the name, a nod to Ben Wyvis and the northern hills. The small black pup chose her and, soon after, his sister Edal joined the fold when her original home fell through.

Wyvis is the rogue – dark, glossy, fond of ditches and chasing pheasants, he is allergic to traffic. Edal (Eedie when she's sweet) is the boss – silver, eagle-eyed and entirely uninterested in your opinion. She's got a bark like a foghorn and the instincts of a velociraptor. The hens live behind fencing and, believe me, they know it's for their own good.

In 2021, Edal delivered Mari's first homebred litter – nine pups, born with little warning and even less decorum. "The vet said four," Mari says with a shrug. "She doubled it." Clova arrived with flair – a surprise flurry across the hall rug. The first to be born, she never left. She's the escape artist and toast-ceremony enthusiast who found the gap and got under a brand-new fence the morning we took the photos for this book – and she was not sorry. Then there's Darcie, the youngest – five months old, all flying feet, toe-nibbling, fearless attitude, and a bark you can hear in Thurso.

Mari doesn't do tricks. "I just let them be dogs," she says as the four of them loll on the carpet and keep one eye on the kettle. They're vole hunters, caravan adventurers, woodland wanderers. This little clan are Skye to their bones.

The daily toast ceremony is sacred – four terriers in a quiet semicircle, not a paw out of place. No barking, no begging, no hooliganism – just decorum. "They've more integrity than that," Mari says.

She shows them now and then – not for ribbons, but to support the breed. No Crufts, no chasing titles. But when she does step in the ring – only at Scottish-based shows – she brings liver cake. One sniff of her "high tariff treat" and even the floppier ears stand to attention.

She chose the Skye terrier because they're Scottish, rare and in need of people to love and champion them. Now, settled in Caithness with four dogs stretched out like hairy draught excluders, Mari is exactly where she's meant to be. "I bless the day I decided upon a Skye terrier," she says. And if the dogs could talk – which they absolutely can, just not in English – they'd agree.

SGITHEANACH SECRETS – LIVER CAKE FOR LEGENDS
For dogs only – paws off, humans!

When Mari steps into the show ring, she doesn't carry nerves – she carries a pocketful of her homemade liver cake. Clova, whose ears used to fold like deckchairs, now stands proud the moment the treat bag appears. Making your own fresh and healthy dog treats is easy, and the bonus is you know *exactly* what goes into the mix.

MARI'S LIVER CAKE

INGREDIENTS
500g liver, blitzed to a pulp
250g self-raising flour
250g gram flour
½ tsp baking powder
3 eggs
Water or milk to double egg volume

METHOD
Beat eggs with liquid to double volume.

Mix into liver and add dry ingredients to make a thick batter.

Bake in two 20 cm trays at 180°C for 45–60 mins, reducing to 150°C towards the end.

Cool, slice into 1 cm cubes.

Store in the fridge for three to four days. Freeze the rest.

Find yourself on first-name terms with every dog in a 100-mile radius.

Mari recommends halving the recipe the first time.
"It's raw liver — not for the faint-hearted. But dogs love it."

THE TARSKAVAIG SKYES

With Bella and Tessie at his side, Neil is reviving a legacy on the land his family has called home since the late 1600s. In the crofting village of Tarskavaig, where the Cuillin range is best viewed with a Skye terrier at your heels, Neil is quietly rebuilding something precious – something Sgitheanach.

For him, dogs are central to life. A passionate advocate for rare and traditional breeds, Neil has loved bearded collie types and Skye terriers alike, and he holds fast to a core belief – that the animals who live with us should suit the place where we bide. In Skye, where the terrain can be tough and the weather ever changeable, for Neil, there's no better fit than the island dogs.

Skye terriers once roamed the crofts, moors and ridges with intent, their heads held low and proud, but their numbers have dwindled. Fortunately, Neil had a direct line to the breed's local legacy; in the village of Tarskavaig, Maggie MacDonald-Cross made her mark, breeding Skyes of such quality that the pawprints of her dogs now trace across every continent. Maggie's daughter Sarah still lives in the village (she's actually a relative of Neil's), and it was through their support that he was able to get Bella – aka Headscrook Going Home to Tarskavaig. It's a name that says it all.

Bella was a revelation – bold and brilliant – a mirror of Neil's own sense of renewal as he entered his forties. "They say your dog reflects your personality," Neil confides with a grin, "and I believe it's true." Bella brought with her energy and purposefulness, and once she was settled, it was time to find her a companion. With a wider grin, Neil acknowledges it's rare that anyone has just one Skye.

Enter Riskerytree the Countess, with the pet name Tessie, a gentle soul with a bloodline that can be traced to Norfolk, now restored to her island heritage. Between them, Bella and Tessie form a canine yin and yang.

Their first outing on the show scene came at the Skye Terrier Homecoming Show on the island itself, judged by American expert Mr Eugene Zaphiris. Bella impressed in the ring and was described as "very promising". Neil was over the moon, while Tessie, too young to compete, seemed to bask in the adoration of the crowd. As the smallest puppy in the room, she was passed from arm to arm like the most precious bundle of joy. "Skye terriers are so rare," Neil reflects, "that each puppy is celebrated by everyone with a connection to the breed. At my first show, that was the feeling that stayed with me – it was something momentous."

Bella's success continued, and within

the year she'd qualified for Crufts. So, the following spring, Neil and Bella made their way to the world's biggest dog show – a green-carpeted stage where every step is a learning curve. "Each show is a reflection," Neil says. "You think about what worked, where you can improve. It's never the same twice."

At shows, Neil carries with him a piece of advice given by a friend, two decades ago. *Don't follow what the champions are doing. Trust your instinct. Use the best gift you have – your eye. Be super critical of the animals you've got because then you'll know what to look for in others to improve your own.*

At home on the croft, his dogs are far more than showpieces. "They're the guardians of the gate," he says proudly. "Nothing moves without those dark eyes knowing." These terriers patrol five acres of rough and brambled terrain. Their instinct utterly on point, every muscle is shaped by generations bred to endure.

Neil doesn't cut corners. The girls are seen every three months by a top animal physiotherapist, and any niggles are met with a blend of herbal medicine and complementary care. He's even working with a canine nutritionist – always with an eye towards preserving health and strength.

"I'm hugely blessed to have the expertise of Maggie MacDonald-Cross and Sine Threlfall (a Skye-based author who wrote the comprehensive history of the breed) to fall back on," Neil says. "These two women are experts and leave a legacy for the Skye terrier. They learned their knowledge from breeders who kept the dogs alive through two world wars and kept them true to type." For Neil, to follow in their footsteps is an honour and a duty. "There are many breeders whose dogs will never touch the rugged land that shaped this breed. I'm absolutely dedicated to producing dogs true to the spirit of Skye."

Now, there is something new on the horizon. Neil hopes to soon welcome a litter of puppies – the first Skye terrier pups born on the island in more than four decades. It's his dream to walk into the next Skye Homecoming Show with a homebred pup at his side.

"I don't quite know what it is about Skye terriers," he admits, "why they bind to us the way they do." He's asked others, those who've known the breed a lifetime, and there's no easy answer. Maybe the Skye terrier is, like the island itself, just a little elusive – and all the more extraordinary for it.

HIGHLANDER IN MINIATURE

The West Highland White Terrier

BREED STANDARD

GENERAL APPEARANCE: Compact, strongly built, with a deep chest, straight back and a jaunty tail.
COAT: Double coat with a soft, dense undercoat and a harsh, straight outer coat.
COLOUR: White.
EYES: Dark, medium-sized and deeply set with an intelligent expression.
MOVEMENT: Free, straight and powerful with good drive from the hindquarters.
TEMPERAMENT: Friendly, confident, spirited and self-reliant.

ARGYLLSHIRE PRIDE

Small in stature but mighty in spirit, the West Highland white terrier has a presence far greater than its diminutive size. With a quick step and a quizzical twinkle in its dark eyes, the Westie carries itself as confidently as any big dog. This wee terrier, cloaked in snowy white, is among the most recognisable of Scotland's breeds – a cheerful little Highlander that has made its way from the rolling hills of Argyll to family homes around the world. They are spirited and loving, stubborn when the mood takes them and deeply loyal. Each one of these little rascals has a big personality and is utterly proud of it.

Being an Argyllshire man myself, you could not grow up in this bonnie nook of Scotland without spotting them often: trotting along harbour walls, nose to the wind, curled up by roaring fires or nipping round granny's garden on patrol. They're part of the community here, the landscape and our lives.

Westies are strongly built, with a deep chest, sturdy legs and a gleeful carrot-like tail that's usually held upright. Bred to work underground and in craggy country, they are hardy and agile. A halo of harsh white fur frames their face, accentuating inquisitive eyes and the black button nose. One moment you'll find them snuggled on the sofa, the next they're on high alert at the presence of a scurrying squirrel. Ever aware, these nosy wee souls are the perfect watchdog. The Westie's charm has won the breed admirers from kings to common folk, and created a story as bold and textured as the brilliant white coat they sport so proudly.

TEMPERAMENT – BIG DOG, SMALL BODY

These terriers brim with confidence, greeting the world with cheer, ready to chase every rustle in the bushes or announce visitors at the door. Bred as independent hunters, Westies like to make their own decisions – sometimes to their owner's amusement or frustration – yet they balance their boldness with a sunny friendliness. Where a Scottie might watch new people with indifference, a well-socialised Westie often bounces forward, tail wagging, ready to make a new pal.

At home with their family, they are affectionate, lively companions, often wonderful with children if treated respectfully. Compared to their terrier relatives, Westies are perhaps a little more stubborn than Cairns and a bit more outgoing than the at times reserved Skye.

Full of spirit, Westies aren't usually quarrelsome. They'll get along well with other dogs if properly introduced, though their old earthdog instincts run

GROUP: Terrier.
STATUS: Secure, despite numbers dipping.
ORIGIN: Hailing from Argyllshire, this hardy and unmistakeable little terrier was developed from white Cairns to hunt vermin and warn families of strangers approaching.
HEIGHT: Approximately 28 cm at the shoulder.
WEIGHT: Male: 7–10 kg. Female: 6–9 kg.

Socialisation
Friendliness
Trainability

Size

Colour

The West Highland White Terrier

four-legged darlings. But I may be biased, if only a little.

GROOMING & CARE

One glance at a Westie's fluffy white coat and you might worry that they'll be high maintenance but, in truth, their grooming needs are moderate. Westies have a double coat: a harsh outer layer and a soft, dense undercoat, built to shrug off Highland weather.

Most Westies today are clipped, though traditional hand-stripping helps retain the coat's weatherproof qualities. Baths should be occasional, but that depends if they have been splashing in deep puddles! Grooming time is the perfect opportunity to check their ears, teeth and skin, especially as Westies can be prone to minor allergies. A well-groomed Westie is a cheery sight – and they'll happily lap up the attention (and the treats) that come with it.

Exercise is equally important for these plucky wee adventurers. A healthy Westie thrives on around an hour a day – be it a brisk walk, games or a sniffing expedition. That said, many could happily go all day long – up the glen, around the loch, over hills and down to the coast – never tiring nor grumbling. Endlessly upbeat and remarkably amiable, they're always game for a grand ploy. Agility activities suit them beautifully too, but

deep. Small pets may trigger their prey drive, and outside they are enthusiastic explorers, while indoors, they are mostly calm. They're happiest curled at your feet, playing with a favourite toy or joining you for the day's chores, contented to be chumming along with you and more than likely sticking their snout in!

Despite their independent spirit, Westies are not loners. They thrive on love, companionship and a life at the heart of family bustle. In fact, they are training a Westie calls for patience and humour. As with other terriers, any hint of harshness will invite rebellion. A positive, playful approach will bring out their adaptable, willing side.

FROM POLTALLOCH WITH LOVE

Long before they were the more pampered pets we enjoy today, Westies were out rooting through the bracken and briars of Argyll. Like all the terrier crew, they were bred to hunt vermin and keep working land clear of troublesome pests. I'm fairly sure they also served as an active form of doorbell – letting the family know whenever guests were about to arrive for a cèilidh. Listen out, and you'll hear their suspicious warning bark – "juh juh". In fact, someone once told me *not* to name a Westie pup "Joe" as the sound of that particular name echoes the sound of that particular bark!

Their day job of old wasn't glamorous; it was gritty and sometimes dangerous. These dogs would tackle foxes, rats and otters, fearless in pursuit of their quarry. Yet, for generations, many Highlanders believed a white terrier was a weaker pup. Then, dark-coated terriers were preferred for work and a white pup in a litter might even be culled, thought unfit for the hard life underground where camouflage and grit mattered most. Still, the colour trait persisted; its thread of ivory running through the terse woolly

> **DID YOU KNOW?**
> **BITE-SIZED WESTIE**
> - **What's in a Name?:** Westies were once known as "Poltalloch terriers" or "Roseneath terriers" before being recognised by the Kennel Club as the West Highland white terrier in 1907.
> - **Westies in the Trenches:** During the First World War, Westies served as message carriers and vermin controllers in the British trenches.
> - **Westminster Wins:** Westies have won Best in Show twice. In 1942 by Wolvey Pattern of Edgerstoune and in 1962 by Elfinbrook Simon.
> - **Best in Show at Crufts:** 1976 by Dianthus Buttons; 1990 by Olac Moon Pilot; and 2016 by Burneze Geordie Girl.
> - **Carrot Tail:** That iconic tail was designed for grip: it enabled handlers to pull the dog from burrows if needed.

coats of Scotland's terriers, waiting for its moment.

Interestingly, before the West Highland white terrier was formally recognised as a breed in its own right, white puppies from Cairn terrier lines might be registered as Westies. It wasn't until 1924 that the Kennel Club closed this loophole, establishing distinct breed standards and putting an end to cross-registration.

Local legends abound regarding the emergence of this hardy breed. Colonel Edward Donald Malcolm – the sixteenth Laird of Poltalloch – is most often credited for the groundwork that's shaped the modern Westie. Malcolm kept a pack of hard-working terriers – probably Cairn type in stature – at his estate in Argyll for dispatching rabbits, rats and foxes. The story goes, the colonel experienced a hunter's worst horror, mistaking one of his reddish-brown dogs for a fox during an evening shoot, as the daylight was getting low. Losing his favourite dog in the shooting accident, a saddened Malcolm vowed never again to risk such a mistake. From then on, he would buck convention and breed only white dogs that could be easily distinguished against the landscape, especially in poor light conditions. Thus his line of Poltalloch terriers came into being, with no fear of a fight in the dark.

Malcolm's white terriers quickly proved their worth, and word of their prowess spread through the network of grand houses. By the turn of the twentieth century, they were appearing at dog shows – often still listed under the name "White Scottish terriers". True to his modest nature, Colonel Malcolm refused to have the breed named after himself or his estate and, in 1903, he made it clear that these terriers should not carry the Poltalloch name. The following year, a breed club was established under the patronage of other aristocratic dog lovers; the Duke of Argyll and the Countess of Aberdeen. Though there were discussions about naming the breed the "Argyllshire Terrier", in 1907 the name "West Highland White Terrier" was made official through Kennel Club recognition.

FROM GAME TO FAME

This breed's journey from working life to the cosy comforts of home has not dulled its instincts. The heart of a hunter still beats inside every Westie. The boldness that once sent them down a burrow now sends them boldly towards a much larger dog at the park just to say hello, and they will eagerly and fearlessly run towards any scrap or tussle – not necessarily to join in, but certainly to check it out. The tenacity that kept them digging after a rat for hours now shows itself when determined to get a treat from a kitchen cupboard, locked or otherwise. And part of their appeal, of course, is that courage is matched only by their sense of fun.

To live with a Westie is to be reminded daily of simple joys. It's waking up to a wee face eager for the day. They don't cower or grovel; they meet your gaze with that steady, twinkling look that says, "I'm game if you are." They may test the rules, but they'll also brighten your darkest day with their sense of mischief and their cuddles.

Westies are deeply bonded to their people. They thrive on activity and on belonging: they'll wait patiently at your feet as you cook, shadow you from room to room, overseeing every errand as if it were a matter for parliamentary discussion at Holyrood . . . It's this mix of spirited independence and fierce loyalty that makes them so beloved. That and the undeniable cute factor that's catapulted them into advertising campaigns, TV dramas like *Hamish Macbeth*, and even Gaelic series like my own *Gàrradh Phàdruig*. A Westie loves an audience almost as much as the audience loves them.

Their worldwide popularity has helped protect them from the decline facing some other Scottish breeds, and thankfully Westie numbers remain relatively strong. Long live the bold Westie, the little white lion of the Highlands!

THE WESTIE WHO STOLE TWO HEARTS

Modern dating techniques can leave pawprints on your heart, as Carol, a physio based in Glasgow's Southside, was to discover. She was swiping through profiles when one stopped her in her tracks. It showed a sunlit glen, a handsome and rugged guy with just the cutest face ever. Carol took one look, swooned and thought, *Oh, he's lovely!* She meant the dog, of course – who else? Then she smiled to herself and added, "I wonder if the man's nice too?"

Spoiler alert: he was. Two years later, and Rab the man and Lyle the Westie's bachelor days are firmly behind them, and the trio now split their time between Highland Perthshire and Glasgow. Lyle, it turns out, is as versatile as he is charming. One of the amazing things about Westies is how they can cope with city life or country pursuits with equal zeal.

Their first date set the tone. Carol joined Rab and Lyle for a romantic climb up Ben Vrackie in the snow. They got to know each other on the ascent, shared lunch at the summit with white hills stretching out all around and watched Lyle playing and merging with the snowline as happy as the proverbial dog with two tails. It was joy from the start – apart from one small surprise. When Carol mentioned she was vegetarian, both Rab and Lyle looked at each other, alarmed. Rab adjusted. Lyle remains sceptical!

In the hills, he's in his element – fearless, scruffy and delighted to be tagging along on Rab's forestry and environmental contracting rounds. He bounds through bracken, chases the wind and patrols the glens like a wee hooligan. "He's the ultimate hill dog," says Carol.

"He's absolutely living his best life up there."

But come Monday, it's back to Glasgow, and Lyle flips the switch. Gone is the rugged explorer and in his place is a confident, urbane gent strutting the pavements of the Southside like he owns them. He's a regular in local cafés (particularly fond of a puppuccino) and turns heads wherever he goes. "He's got such presence," Carol laughs. "It's like walking with a tiny celebrity." And she's right: there's something magnetic about Lyle. People are drawn to him – children, old folks, even strangers in the park – and he has a knack for bringing out a smile. Whether welcoming guests, posing for photos, or cocking his head listening to your stories, he carries a natural charm that's hard to ignore.

Like every great Westie, he's got quirks too. Ask him to do something he doesn't fancy, "go to bed", for example, and he'll bolt for the living room in protest. Ask again, and you'll be treated to the world's slowest walk, eyes wide and pleading, pure Bambi. It's his dramatic act of rebellion and it never fails to get a laugh.

Carol had always dreamed of having a Westie. Little did she know one would come as part of a package – and bring so much love and laughter with him. "He's the glue," she says. "The heart of our wee household. We really are a team now – the three of us."

Lyle may have started out as the hook on a dating profile, but he's become much more than that. He's a four-pawed bridge between hill and city, mischief and manners, old routines and new beginnings, between two people who care deeply for each other. A true ambassador for his breed – and for love, in all its unexpected forms.

SKYE – A LITTLE WHITE LIGHT

Skye might be compact, but he carries a whole world of love and loyalty in that sturdy frame. Now five years old, he shares his life with Ian and Brian, who moved to Oban from Wigan in 2023. The move brought a fresh start and, with it, a fresh set of pawprints – those of a West Highland white terrier – in their lives. Having just said goodbye to their old dog, Parson, the guys decided to contact Fiona's Ark, a local rehoming charity just north of Oban.

There they met Skye, then four years old, and instantly knew he was the one. A short walk together sealed the deal. "He took to us straight away," Ian remembers. Just two weeks later, Skye moved in. He's been their shadow ever since.

What drew them to him wasn't just his size (perfect for a flat) or his dapper looks – it was his temperament. "Loving, lively and loyal," Ian says, and it's clear that Skye's character runs deep. He's alert but gentle, spirited but sensitive. He's even known to offer a comforting cuddle when Ian or Brian are feeling low. "He listened when I told him about Parson," Ian says softly. "I think he understood."

In line with his thoughtful nature, Skye is a proud Pets As Therapy dog, visiting hospitals, care homes and dementia centres where he has a knack for making people smile. "He enjoys a good laugh with the residents," Ian exclaims. "He really knows how to read the room." He's particularly gentle with less able people and, when invited, will hop up on a lap to offer a soft presence and a snuggle.

At home, Skye is a fantastic companion who keeps close watch – he sleeps at the foot of the bed, keeps tabs on the postie and can always sniff out an empty seat. But his favourite is when it's time to hit the beach at Ganavan; there, he runs like a rabbit, full of energy and joy. As Ian and Brian testify, life really is better with a Westie!

fionasark.org.uk

PRIDE OF SCOTLAND

The Scottish Terrier

BREED STANDARD

GENERAL APPEARANCE: Compact, powerful, low to the ground with a dignified bearing.
COAT: Hard, wiry outer coat with a dense, soft undercoat.
COLOUR: Black, wheaten or brindle.
EYES: Piercing, almond-shaped, dark brown and expressive.
MOVEMENT: Free, smooth and powerful for such a short frame.
TEMPERAMENT: Bold, independent, self-assured, yet deeply loyal.

PROUD BY NATURE

They may be short, but their spirit is not and their fame stretches as wide as the Grampian range. Bold of heart, somewhat rascally, with a glint in their eye and a strut that says they are nobody's fool – that's the iconic Scottish terrier.

If Scotland is known for whisky, kilts and haggis, then none are quite as emblematic of our wee country as this braw powerhouse of a dog. For me, it's a toss-up between the Scottish terrier and the Highland cow for the crown of Scotland's most post-carded icon – and the black Scottie probably edges it! These wee dogs possibly do more for tourism than the Loch Ness Monster, and I dare say you are far likelier to spot the former than the latter, despite their rarity!

The Scottie doesn't try to be liked – they simply are. Known for being entirely uninterested in flattery, they are the very embodiment of Caledonian dignity: humble yet formidable. Like the skirl of bagpipes, they're hard to ignore. Aye, they are a wee dog who knows exactly who they are.

This no-nonsense terrier has charmed monarchs, movie stars, presidents and whisky connoisseurs. Rugged yet refined, reserved yet beloved, independent yet deeply loyal, few dogs epitomise such paradox as these punky Scottish patriots in miniature.

TEMPERAMENT

This is a courageous, independent and self-assured little dog. In fact, breed historians note the Scottish terrier may be even more tenacious and feistier than all the other terriers combined. That said, aggression is absolutely not the goal – a well-bred Scottie will be bold but never ill-tempered. They are vigilant watch-dogs, typically reserved with strangers, but not too quick to sound an alert, so you shouldn't be lumbered with yapping – in theory!

Amid their family, Scotties are deeply loving in their own understated way. They tend to form a tight bond with one or two people – often choosing their human and following them like a bairn trailing contentedly after their granny. A Scottie is loyal to a fault to their special someone. Don't expect fawning affection or slobbery kisses, but do expect a constant, watchful presence at your side. They are highly intelligent, but unlike, say, a golden retriever, they are not eager to please simply for the sake of it.

Around the home, Scotties are generally calm, steady companions, happy to snooze in their favourite spot – often somewhere that gives them a good vantage point to supervise the household. Despite their serious expression, many are quite the clown in private. You'll soon discover why they're famous for

GROUP: Terrier.
STATUS: Formally "at watch" due to a worrying decline.
ORIGIN: From the North East, the Scottish terrier was bred for tenacity in hunting vermin across rugged farmland and estates and earned its distinct identity by the late 19th century.
HEIGHT: 25 cm at the withers.
WEIGHT: 8.5–10.5 kg.

Socialisation
Friendliness
Trainability

Size

Colour

the "Scottie Blitz", in which they'll tear around the house at full speed, tail flying, just for the sheer heck of it.

However, joking aside, a Scottie won't tolerate being manhandled or teased and, for this reason, many folk say Scotties are best suited to adult households, or families with older, respectful children who understand a dog's boundaries.

Another important aspect is their strong prey drive. This dog was bred to chase and dig; if it's small and runs – whether a squirrel, rat, rabbit or the neighbour's cat – a Scottie will likely pursue it. When a Scottie decides to give chase, their hearing all but shuts off, and no amount of calling will bring them back until they're good and ready.

LOOKING AFTER YOUR SCOTTIE

There's a reason these terriers will turn heads like a handsome man in full Highland dress. That crisp beard, the flowing kilt of fur on the belly, the perky eyebrows . . . all give an almost aristocratic air. But, just as with their human counterparts, that iconic look doesn't happen by itself.

The breed has a harsh, wiry double

coat designed to repel dirt and water, and care of it is a big part of Scottie maintenance. Properly groomed, a Scottie's coat doesn't shed much hair and will keep its coarse texture. To maintain it, the outer coat needs to be hand-stripped several times a year. Most Scottie owners use a professional groomer familiar with terriers, as their trimmed look – particularly the beard and furnishings – is not easy to achieve at home.

On the exercise front, Scotties are a little easier than some of their terrier clan. They are energetic but not hyper, and don't require endless hours of activity to be happy. A healthy adult usually thrives on a couple of short twenty-minute walks each day. In hot weather, it's best to be cautious. They are built close to the ground and, especially if dark coated, Scotties can overheat quickly. Keep them comfortable by offering plenty of shade, fresh water and avoiding the midday sun.

One of the heartening things about the breed is their longevity. Scottish terriers are hardy, robust dogs and they often age gracefully, retaining their dignified posture and keen expression well into their teens. Owners frequently note how their Scottie will remain active and spirited until very late in life – albeit, like the best of us, a little grey round the whiskers.

> **DID YOU KNOW?**
> **BITE-SIZED SCOTTIE**
> - **An Older Name:** In the early nineteenth century, Scottish terriers were often called Aberdeen terriers, named for the Granite City and surrounding areas where the type was particularly common.
> - **Monopoly Piece:** The little dog player piece in the classic Monopoly board game is a Scottie; added in 1942, it has since become the players' favourite.
> - **Star of the Silver Screen:** A Scottish terrier made a splash in *Lady and the Tramp* (1955), with the dapper Jock stealing scenes as Lady's pal and the voice of good sense. With his rolling brogue and old-fashioned manners, Jock gave cinemagoers a picture-perfect Scottie.
> - **Naming a Nation's Terrier:** Captain Gordon Murray was instrumental with his breeding, honing many distinct characteristics of the dogs we know today. He is believed to have named them "Scottish Terriers" in 1879.

DEEP ROOTS IN ROUGH GROUND

The Scottish terrier is a breed hewn from the northeast of Scotland. Born among the burrows and cairns of rural Aberdeenshire, harsh weather was a constant trial and vermin an inevitable foe.

Their true origins are far older than any pedigree; before the Kennel Club, show ring, breed standards or Crufts, there were simply "Scotch terriers" – rough-coated working dogs tasked with the elimination of pests. Each region bred dogs to match its own terrain, and in Scotland's Doric lands these distinctive dogs emerged.

By the early 1800s, they were getting themselves noticed beyond their working role. Writers like Sir Walter Scott – who kept a proto-Scottie or Cairn-like terrier called Camp – helped to romanticise Scotland's native terriers. Yet it wasn't until the late nineteenth century that the dog we now know as the Scottish terrier truly began to take shape.

Through the work of fanciers like J. B. Morrison and W. L. McCandlish, the Scottie was standardised, as its wiry coat, upright ears and dignified bearing codified into breed lore. The first breed club was founded in 1882, and by the twentieth century, the Scottie had become one of the best-loved dogs in Britain.

> ## CHAMPIONS OF SCOTTIES
> **J. B. Morrison** – Known as "Mr Scott Terrier", he developed the early bloodlines that would shape the modern Scottish terrier.
>
> **W. L. McCandlish** – He refined the Scottie's form and spirit, authoring one of the first great breed books – *The Scottish Terrier*, which was published in 1909.

FASHION, FAME & THE WHISKY PAIR

No discussion of the Scottie would be complete without a toast to Black & White whisky. In the 1890s, James Buchanan – one of the great whisky barons – needed a symbol to distinguish his brand. After seeing a dog show at London's Crystal Palace, he chose the contrast of two terriers – a black Scottie and a white Westie. It was a marketing masterstroke in which the duo of dogs became instantly recognisable, undeniably Scottish mascots. The pairing spoke to taste, tradition and national identity – appearing on adverts, labels and bar mirrors around the world. For millions, they became the very symbol of Scotland.

THE SCOTTIE GOES TO WASHINGTON

There's no denying it: the Scottish terrier has a nose for power. Not content with strutting its stuff through the glens and drawing rooms of Scotland, this doughty little dog made its way across the Atlantic to the most famous house of all to claim its place beneath the Oval Office desk – and all with the understated confidence of a ghillie who's just spotted a fine ten-pointer stag!

The most iconic of all was Fala – or, to give him his full name, Murray the Outlaw of Falahill – who belonged to none other than President Franklin D. Roosevelt. Far more than a pet, he was practically a cabinet member, travelling with the president on official business. He even attracted his own press coverage and once became the subject of a biting political rumour, which famously led Roosevelt to defend him: "You can criticise me, my wife and my family, but you can't criticise my little dog." Everyone listening lapped it up. And Fala was so beloved that he was cast in bronze beside Roosevelt at the FDR Memorial in Washington, DC. A mere stone's throw from greatness, tail forever curled, there he sits, immortalised as one of America's First Dogs.

But Fala wasn't the only Scottie to hold court at the White House. Fast forward to the early 2000s, and enter Barney stage right, another perky black Scottie with a presidential gleam in his eye. George W. Bush was the man in charge, but it was Barney who ran the show. Every Christmas, the nation tuned in to Barney Cam, a seasonal video diary of life in the White House from a Scottie's-eye view. One year he inspected the decorations, another year he interviewed Cabinet members. All without saying a word, but conveying very definite meaning with a raise of those eyebrows!

Barney was soon joined by Miss Beazley, and then there were two Scotties in the West Wing. A gift to First Lady Laura Bush, the pair made quite the power couple – dignified, alert and

---

THE WATCHLIST

To safeguard breeds of British and Irish origin that are considered at risk of disappearing, the Kennel Club created the "vulnerable native breeds" list – those with fewer than 300 registrations a year – and the "at watch" list, for those with between 300 and 450 registrations a year, in order that the situation may be monitored.

SCOTLAND'S ENDANGERED SIX

Of the Scottish dogs currently designated "vulnerable" there are six breeds: the bearded collie, the smooth collie, the Dandie Dinmont terrier, the Gordon setter, the Scottish deerhound and the Skye terrier.

unfazed by the din of politics. There were photo shoots on the lawn, official portraits and walkabouts on Air Force One.

The Scottie's spell, of course, isn't limited to presidents. (Even Dwight D. Eisenhower, back in his military days, had a Scottie named Telek, though by the time he was in the White House, he'd swapped dogs for Heidi the Weimaraner.) A surprising number of cultural icons also tend to fall for the breed's wiry charm. Hollywood legend Humphrey Bogart kept several Scotties. Bette Davis had one called Tibby, who famously had her own chair on set – look up the 1938 photographs of Tibby with Bette and Errol Flynn during a break in filming *The Sisters*. Author Rudyard Kipling wrote very fondly of his Scotties, and Jackie Kennedy had one too – as a child, long before the White House, when she was still just Jacqueline Bouvier, she was photographed walking her Scottie, Hootchie, in New York's Central Park.

No wonder the Americans took to them, though: a dog that looks like a little cask of whisky on legs, acts like a wee chieftain and doesn't suffer fools gladly. If ever there were a breed born for high office, it's the Scottie. Short in leg, long in legacy.

ENDANGERED NOBILITY

Despite its fame, the Scottish terrier is now at risk. In 2024, the Kennel Club placed the breed on its "at watch" list, with only 387 puppies registered in the UK, which feels like a surprising fall from grace for such a storied companion.

How can this happen to a dog so beloved? Partly, it's fashion – trends shift and the modern appetite for "designer" breeds has sidelined many of our heritage dogs. The Scottie's stoic temperament can also be misunderstood in a world that prizes eager affection and constant interaction.

Those who know the breed know its worth: a dog that stands by your side and who is loyal without being needy. But, of course, they do need you. Breed clubs, enthusiasts and heritage campaigns are now working to reverse the decline – not just for Scotties, but for all these vulnerable dogs. Now is the time to celebrate the Scottie's special place in Scotland's story and in the hearts of families across the world. Who knows, perhaps you will consider one as your home's new companion?

A KILT OF SCOTTIES – THE NORTHERN PACK

It was early morning on the outskirts of Oban; the sun was beginning to tip the hills with gold, and mist still clung low over Ben Cruachan in the distance. That's when I saw them. The two women striding up the croft track, visiting friends bound for island holiday adventures with a kilt of Scotties at their heels – and equally faithful husbands not far behind!

Fliss and Olwen are great pals, united by their love of Scottish terriers, bonded through windy walks with the most striking pack of Scotties you ever saw! They were on their way to Mull for a week-long break – dogs and all. They agreed to come and meet me first thing for a walk, and what a sight they made. A troupe of darting wee black legs – and a wheaten one, too – tails high, noses down in the early morning dew. You can't look at them and not smile – that's the irresistible power of dogs – and even more so, a full canine clan.

Olwen lives in North Tyneside with her husband Kevin, near the long beaches and shifting skies where Northumberland meets the North Sea. Retired, she now spends her days exploring coast paths and forest trails with her constant companion, Brèagha. Officially Tonilea Queen of Kings, Brèagha was the only girl in a litter of boys, and she carries herself like royalty.

"She's my shadow," says Olwen. "She's beside me every step. I don't even need to call – she's already there." Calm, poised, regal and bonnie just like her name, Brèagha is the group's peacekeeper. If play gets too rowdy, a low growl from her settles it at once. "She never needs to follow it up," Olwen smiles. "She's got that voice. Just like my Scottish granny; she'd say 'now, mind' and that was enough."

Fliss, meanwhile, lives further south in County Durham with her husband Nick and a terrier household so lively it probably needs its own weekly newsletter. There's Radley and Dougal – cheeky litter brothers from Bobelmia lines – followed by siblings Fergus and Brodie. Then came another brother, Hamish, who joined the fold after his previous owner passed away. Collectively they were known, for a time, as *The Wingate Five* – but not for long.

Just as I thought I'd met the whole tribe, Fliss unzipped her bag and – like a magician producing a rabbit from a hat – lifted out a tiny twelve-week-old Scottie pup, Effie. Kenbloom Wrong Sister by pedigree; Euphemia Martha when up to mischief. The wee cutie blinked at the world, took in the hill, the sea air, the herd of Scottie uncles, and then nestled straight back into Fliss's arms.

My heart melted as I swooned, and I tried to steal her – I really did – but she already only had eyes for Fliss. That's the Scottie way: loyal beyond measure, fierce in their affections and forever devoted to their chosen folk. Like so many of our Scottish dogs, you don't get a Scottie's heart without earning it, and once you have it, they're yours for life.

Olwen and Fliss met through the North East England Scottie Group – an extended family of sorts, where over thirty Scotties might gather for a single walk, snuffling and strutting like a furry platoon on a mission. Their friendship, like their dogs, is steady, full of spirit and rooted in something deeply shared. "We just get each other," says Olwen. "It's not just about the dogs – it's the stories, the support, the sense of belonging."

And so it was. A damp dawn walk on the outskirts of Oban, a moment in time so rare it felt like an opening scene from a *Katie Morag* story – the holidaymakers with seven Scotties! It was a walk I will never forget. As I watched the troop stroll down the hill towards the ferry in the harbour, I chuckled. *What a sight to behold! The Muileachs don't know what's coming. That indomitable lot*, I thought, *will stop the traffic in Tobermory.*

A LITTLE DOG BY A LITTLE BAY

Hamish the Scottish terrier may have been born in Wales in August 2021, but he found his forever home in Argyll just a few months later. Norman and his wife Pat adopted him in March 2022 through the Scottish Terrier Emergency Care Scheme (STECS), a long-established, volunteer-run charity dedicated to the rescue, rehoming and welfare of Scotties across the UK. STECS arranged for Hamish to travel north by train, and the handover took place over a cup of coffee across from Glasgow Central station. This marked an informal but heartfelt beginning to what has become a very happy match.

As a pup, Hamish embraced all the classic Scottie antics – joyfully chewing the post, stealing spectacles and tipping over his water bowl with reckless joy. These days, he's mellowed into a funny wee character who brings delight to the household, though the mischief hasn't entirely vanished. He adores tearing up cardboard boxes and sheets of paper, and he's obsessed with balls – in fact, no toy is too small, no game too long. The terrier instinct runs strong when it comes to treasure – Hamish is known to bury his treats like a wee canine pirate, hiding them in the garden or, more cheekily, in the bed or down the back of the settee.

Though he's a homebody at heart and rarely strays, this guy is still a terrier through and through. He's affectionate, independent, obedient enough (when it suits him) and a master of evasion if he senses a grooming brush or a tick inspection approaching. Catching him in those moments can feel like a game of wits – in which Hamish has a fighting chance of outwitting you. He seems to know, though, what a lucky pup he is, to find such an Oban-minded family, willing to offer a rescue dog a fresh start by the sea.

Underneath the Scottie stubbornness lies a deeply contented dog, rooted in a life that suits him well. Hamish has settled into the rhythms of Oban life – watching the ferries coming and going, pottering along the shore and making regular appearances on the town's pavements like a pocket-sized, bewhiskered dignitary. This familiar face on the esplanade is a fine ambassador for his breed.

Norman hopes his dog's story reminds others that adopting a rescue doesn't necessarily mean turning your back on Scotland's native breeds. Whether through charities like STECS or other breed-specific rehoming groups, it's entirely possible to give a second chance to a dog with native heritage.

stecs.net

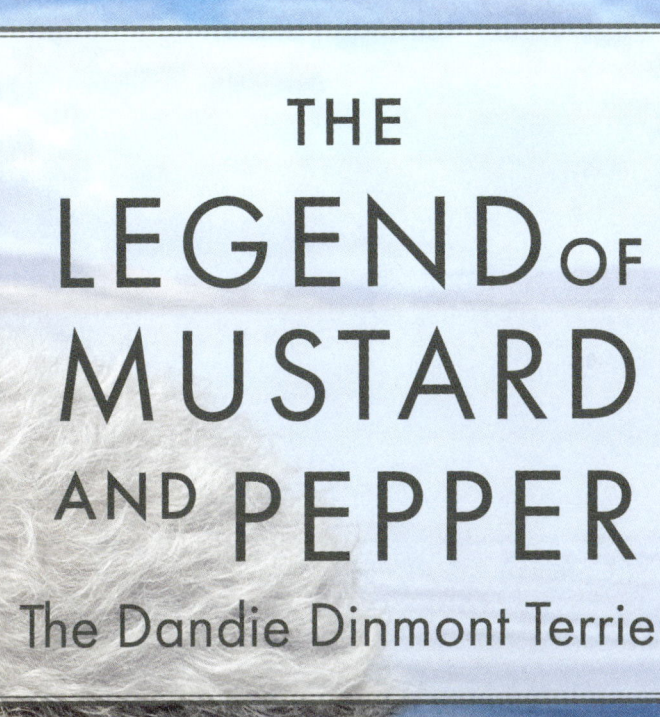

THE LEGEND OF MUSTARD AND PEPPER

The Dandie Dinmont Terrier

BREED STANDARD

GENERAL APPEARANCE: Distinctive long, low body, muscular with a soft, wise expression.
COAT: Double coat with soft, linty undercoat and harder topcoat, 5 cm long, not wiry but crisp, profuse soft top knot.
COLOUR: Pepper (bluish black to silvery grey, silvery white top knot) or mustard (reddish brown to pale fawn, creamy white top knot).
EYES: Large, round, rich hazel – full of intelligence.
MOVEMENT: Free, effortless, ground-covering stride.
TEMPERAMENT: Independent, dignified, determined and affectionate.

CHARACTER IN EVERY INCH

The Dandie Dinmont terrier's confident, jaunty air is unmistakable: long-bodied, flexible and yet barely off the ground, they carry surprising heft in a small frame. Their distinctive coat is a crisp mix of hard and soft hairs known as piley, which makes it very weatherproof. The head is dramatically crowned by a soft top knot, the trademark characteristic of these loveable dogs. The domed skull, wide-set hazel eyes and expressive face give the Dandie an intelligent, almost wistful charm. Large, pendulous ears frame the face, while the round, shovel-like paws remind us that this is no ornamental dog – every feature speaks of centuries of hard work and incredible digging prowess. They have powerful jaws with strong teeth, especially the canines, which are extraordinarily big for a smaller dog.

TEMPERAMENT & LIVING WITH A DANDIE

Unlike the frenetic nature of some terrier breeds, the Dandie is generally a touch more reserved. They tend to be calm, pensive companions who are content to curl up under a table, chill behind the sofa or gaze peaceably out the window, rather than bounce off the walls. They form deep attachments to their family and are extremely affectionate.

No matter how polished their appearance, Dandies have never forgotten their roots – or their burrowing instincts. Whether it's a molehill in a meadow, a sandy beach or the loose soil of a garden bed, a Dandie sets to it with its powerful forelegs to excavate. They will almost certainly trot back from the garden with a muddy snout and even muddier paws, very pleased with themselves for having made such a big old mess! They are loyal watchdogs with a deep, loud bark that's surprising for their size – a Dandie will sound the alarm if someone comes to the door, but they tend not to be chronic yappers. Typically, they'll only bark when there is real cause.

Theirs is a warm presence which will want to be near you; as a puppy, you can expect an affectionate dog who likes frequent cuddles. Their loyalty runs deep, and they are very sensitive. Be sure, of course, to always be consistent and kind: they will remember, and not necessarily forgive, any harsh treatment. Such is the characterful nature of this wise and wily dog.

EXERCISE & ACTIVITY NEEDS

Dandies don't need lots of intense exercise; an hour or so a day, including some off-lead running or scent-based play, is usually enough. They love to explore and use their noses – no surprises there; after

GROUP: Terrier.
STATUS: Vulnerable.
ORIGIN: Emerging in the early 1700s in the border region between Scotland and England, the Dandie Dinmont terrier was developed for hunting otters and badgers.
HEIGHT: 20–28 cm at the shoulder.
WEIGHT: 8–11 kg.

> **DID YOU KNOW?**
> **BITE-SIZED DANDIE**
> - **Literary Namesake:** The Dandie Dinmont terrier is the only dog breed named after a fictional character. In his novel *Guy Mannering*, Sir Walter Scott created "Dandie Dinmont" – the owner of a pack of these working terriers who, thanks to the book's huge popularity, lent his name to the breed.
> - **Oldest Bloodlines:** Every pedigree Dandie Dinmont terrier alive descends from a single dog – Old Ginger from Selkirk. A bronze statue of Old Ginger now stands at The Haining in Selkirk where he was born.

all, they are so low to the ground! They are robustly burly and are really rather agile and athletic when on the move. Dandies are highly intelligent, extremely playful, and their balanced temperament makes them wonderful with children and adults alike.

GROOMING & CARE

The Dandie's coat does need fairly regular attention. A weekly brush – more during shedding seasons – keeps the crisp twin texture in good condition. Many owners choose to hand-strip the coat every few months – this really is a skill, for which I recommend you find a professional groomer who knows the art of stripping – to maintain its look and feel. Having said that, I know many people with a Dandie who have learned to strip their own dog's hair very well – practice makes perfect! Their top knot can be trimmed gently to stay neat, and their ears should be checked regularly. They are minimal shedders, are generally clean dogs and rarely need a bath, unless, of course, they've rolled in something foul – which, being terriers, they might just do!

FROM FICTION TO FAME

The Dandie Dinmont terrier's tale has its origins in the Borders in the 1700s. For generations, farmers and gentlemen had bred local terriers, keeping

> **DID YOU KNOW?**
> **BITE-SIZED DANDIE**
> - **Sir Alec Guinness & His Dandie:** Famed for so many roles, including Obi-Wan Kenobi, the actor shared his life with a Dandie. He may have played a Jedi Master on screen, but at home, the force was strong with the Dandie.
> - **A Tartan of Their Own:** The Dandie holds a truly unique honour, being the only dog breed permitted to wear an official Scottish tartan. In 2015, with the blessing of the Duke of Buccleuch, who is also chief of Clan Scott, the breed adopted Sir Walter Scott Black & White tartan.
> - **Madison Square Garden Marvel:** The Dandie Dinmont terrier has made its mark at the Westminster Kennel Club Dog Show in New York. In 1993, Pennywise the Butler Did It won the Terrier Group. Then in 2007, Hobergays Fineus Fogg repeated the achievement, proving that the Dandies really do turn heads in the ring.

these low-bodied, strong-jawed dogs to dispatch vermin of all sizes. They were prized for courage and cleverness alongside their adorable looks.

One renowned terrierman, James Davidson of Hindlee, kept some two dozen such dogs and – with typical Borders humour – gave *all* the pepper-coloured dogs the name Pepper and the light ones Mustard, distinguishing them only by age or size – Auld Pepper, Young Mustard, Little Pepper and so on. Davidson's witty habit was well known in the Borders countryside, but it was about to become known far beyond the Borders, thanks to the pen of Sir Walter Scott.

In 1815, Scotland's great novelist published *Guy Mannering*, and within its pages he included a curly-haired farmer character inspired by Davidson. This fictional farmer was named Dandie Dinmont and, you guessed it, he owned a pack of faithful terriers named Pepper and Mustard. Dandie's pride in his dogs is one of the novel's great enduring charms: he boasts of having *a hantle o' terriers* – a whole lot of terriers – and when asked what brings him pleasure in life, he replies simply and movingly, "Terriers of a guid breed – it's a' the pleasure I hae on yearth."

In Scott's novel, Dandie's no-nonsense wife, Meg, often grumbles about the ever-growing pack, but when

asked about his dogs, Dandie is unwavering in his affection, telling Counsellor Pleydell: "I like them weel eneugh – better, maybe, than the best o' them – for they're ay about me, and ken me, and I ken them." A sentiment many dog lovers would agree with, I'm sure!

Walter Scott had spent time as a sheriff in Selkirkshire, where he would have heard tales of these gritty little terriers, which he then wove into his story. The book became an instant success – remarkably, like a modern-day Taylor Swift gig, it sold out in a day! – and readers were evidently enchanted by Dandie Dinmont and his dogs. All of a sudden, *everyone* wanted one of *Dandie's terriers*. Letters poured into the Borders from lords and ladies offering to buy a pair of those silky, weaselly dogs with the funny names. The demand was so great that Scott's fictional name – Dandie Dinmont's terrier – soon found itself stuck to the real breed. James Davidson himself – the living inspiration for Dinmont – was bemused to find his humble hunting dogs now so very famous. Still, he good-naturedly played along and answered to the nickname Dandie Dinmont for the rest of his days, proud that his beloved Peppers and Mustards had put the Borders on the doggy map.

Long before the novel's publication, though, Davidson had been carefully breeding his terriers and keeping meticulous notes of his pairings, with his lines hailing from local dogs of renown. In a very real sense, he was one of the originators of the modern Dandie Dinmont terrier. Through Scott's tale, the pepper and mustard terriers bounded their rigorous way from farmsteads to fashionable estates, and everywhere in between.

OLD GINGER – FATHER OF A BREED

Walter Scott's connection to the Dandie Dinmont terrier was more than literary. From his home at Abbotsford, his grand estate near Melrose, Scott was part of a lively network of terrier enthusiasts that stretched across what became known as the Selkirk Triangle, a corner of the Borders anchored by Bowhill, The Haining and Abbotsford itself.

In 1842, at the stately property of The Haining in Selkirk, a litter of Dandie Dinmont puppies was born that would change the course of the breed's history. Among them was a pup who came to be known as Old Ginger, and this mustard-hued hound would become the cornerstone of the modern Dandie.

While full pedigrees had yet to be formalised in that era, Old Ginger was the son of the celebrated Old Pepper, another working terrier of some renown whose name echoed the long-standing

habit of being named for the spices. Old Ginger was owned by Mr E. Bradshaw Smith. One of the early champions of the breed, Smith recognised the dog's potential and bred him carefully. And it is his Old Ginger to whom, to this day, every registered Dandie can trace its lineage.

Remarkably, the original kennels where Old Ginger was born still stand at The Haining. In 2017, on the 175th anniversary of his birth, Dandie lovers from around the world gathered there to unveil a life-sized bronze statue in his honour in the very courtyard where he was once whelped.

By the mid-nineteenth century, the Dandie Dinmont terrier had become a fixture both in the field and at shows. In November 1875, enthusiasts formed the Dandie Dinmont Terrier Club at a meeting in the Fleece Hotel in Selkirk – making it one of the oldest surviving breed clubs in the world, and the oldest dedicated to a terrier.

THE ARTFUL DANDIE

Beyond Scott, the visual art of the era also celebrated the breed. In the National Galleries of Scotland hangs a remarkable painting of a Dandie, surely one of the breed's most visible ambassadors. The famous dog painter John Emms created a beloved portrait of "Callum" that vividly

> **DID YOU KNOW?**
> **BITE-SIZED DANDIE**
> - **A Dog by Any Other Name:** Mustard, Pepper, Ginger, Spice and Soy – Sir Walter Scott called his terriers "all the cruets", matching the condiment sets found in Scotland's more refined homes!
> - **Marple & the Muzzle:** Agatha Christie shared her family home with her brother Monty's Dandie Dinmont called Scotty. While Miss Marple solved murders, Scotty snored under the desk – crime-fighting, Dandie-style.

captures the breed's character – a beautiful mustard dog, hardy and fearless, who proudly displays the rat he has just caught.

Yes, they can do that!

Callum belonged to John Cowan Smith, a passionate art collector and dog lover, who left a substantial bequest to the National Galleries in 1919. His gift came with an extraordinary condition – that Callum's portrait remain permanently and prominently displayed. The Callum Bequest, as it became known, still contributes to the gallery's acquisitions today. The curators have kept their promise, elegantly hanging Callum in the gallery, rather thoughtfully placing him slightly lower down the wall, as he is so popular, with children especially. Fittingly, he has been positioned beside a bust of Sir Walter Scott himself – a fine and dandy pair, for sure, delighting visitors who can all enjoy free entry to the galleries' permanent collections.

A GATHERING OF FRIENDS
The Dandie Dinmont Terrier Clubs

Those dedicated to the Dandie Dinmont terrier are determined that this legendary breed will never be lost to history. Across the UK, three devoted breed clubs are working not only to celebrate the Dandie's heritage but to secure its future.

The Dandie Dinmont Terrier Club, the Southern Dandie Dinmont Terrier Club and the Caledonian Dandie Dinmont Terrier Club are each rooted in their own corner of Britain, but they share one common goal. Together, they

champion responsible breeding, health research and public awareness, while fostering community through shows, events and mentoring. There is even a Dandie Dinmont Derby which is a great day out. I won't lie, not all Dandies are built for racing: some race for the finish line, while others bring only hilarity and calamity!

Wonderfully, all three clubs are currently collaborating on a comprehensive census project to better understand the breed's population and ownership across the UK. This joint effort reflects the seriousness of the Dandie's vulnerable status and the absolute commitment within the community.

I am honoured to serve as Patron of the Caledonian Club, which is a gathering of some of the finest, kindest folk you could hope to meet. They are guardians not only of a breed's shape, coat and movement, but, I genuinely believe, of its very soul. The club organises a variety of annual events ranging from grooming masterclasses to social forays, and even matchmaking (of dogs!). These events build skill and knowledge and bring people together. The animals need good people to fight their corner, and it's clear that the dogs enjoy getting together too: there is nothing merrier than a cèilidh of terriers.

So, as I can't say too often, if you find that the dogs of Scotland – the steadfast

terriers and noble hounds of this land – are tugging at your heart, seek out the breed clubs. Among their ranks, you'll find not only good advice, but good company and a warm welcome to a fellowship of four-legged, tail-wagging histories.

After all, when it comes to Dandies, one glance into those deep, wise eyes can win a new admirer on the spot. Take it from me: I speak from experience here! It is worth remembering that if you take on a rare breed, you are very likely to become an ambassador for their kind. In itself, this is an act of love: every dog that finds a new family brings the breed one step closer to stability.

SISTERS IN SPIRIT – PRESERVING A NATIONAL TREASURE

Those forward-facing, soulful eyes that seem to listen when you speak can't help but linger in the memory. They don't just look at you – they *really* see you – and then they blink with mischief, intelligence and a promise of something fun to follow. Yes, these are eyes that can talk!

For Ali of Puddockswell and Angie of Dryfevalley kennels, that depth of perception – along with the Dandie's charm, humour and heart – has kept them devoted to the breed, and as breeders they are the very epitome of what it means to be responsible. Ali has lived alongside Dandies for over forty years, a lifetime of care and commitment woven into every line she's preserved. In 2008, Angie got a pup from her and subsequently joined her in the mission of preservation breeding, and they've since built legacies. Though their kennels are miles apart, and separated by the Irish Sea, their shared purpose has created a genuine kinship. Theirs is a collaboration rooted in a deep love for the Dandie's rare and remarkable character.

"Temperament is paramount," they agree. "We want Dandies who are true to their nature – gentle, spirited, clever

– but also strong in mind and body." That simple mantra has guided not just their own lines, but an international effort to support the breed and aid gene pool diversity. That effort included importing three pups from a litter sired by a champion Dandie belonging to Cathi Tower in the US. The dam was McFlurri, the daughter of Ali's much-loved social media star, @OliveMcDinmont (give her a follow in Instagram). McFlurri now lives a grand life in the mountains of Washington state; she's a reminder that the Dandie story is both deeply Scottish and proudly global. These dogs really are loved the world over.

Our *Tails of Scotland* Dandie photoshoot in Oban was, fittingly, a family affair. There was Thelma – Dryfevalley Jitterbug – a poised seven-year-old matron with a touch of glam in her step – and her cheeky daughter Sissy – Dryfevalley Sassy Lassie, aged two. Morty – Puddockswell Jelly Roll Morton – strode in like a pipe major with a sporran full of high jinks. He's Thelma's half-brother, Sissy's uncle and our Peigi's uncle too – so together we created a proper clan gathering on the Argyllshire coast.

Like all Dandies, they brought personality in spades. They dug holes with gleeful intent, snuffled in corners, unearthed treasures of sticks, shells and crabs – and then they waddled off with their finds like comic book robbers with their swag. Dandies are often downright funny once they trust you; once they feel entirely at home – on your lap, your bed and in your heart – their vivacious characters really shine. They are alert, expressive and present when you talk to them, but the comedy is always there too. Really, how is it that a Dandie can shape-shift from a dainty companion to a ten-tonne weight the moment they sense you're about to pick them up?

But to understand the Dandie's future, just look at the women who stand behind them. When Ali and Angie are with their dogs, there's a softness to the way they smile – a look that tells you everything. "I love all dogs, but Dandies are darlings and razor sharp, too – they always know what is going on," Ali laughs.

"Aye, you are never alone if you have a Dandie," says Angie, chuckling in agreement. "They are nosy wee busybodies."

They adore these animals and, more than that, they understand them – this is something you instinctively know when you encounter happy dogs! I first met Ali and Angie when filming the series for BBC Alba and I found them to be warm, witty and wonderfully pragmatic. They are the sort of women who make the impossible seem entirely achievable. Along with others like them, dotted in quiet pockets around the country, they form a living network of knowledge, wisdom and care.

They are both integral to the Caledonian Dandie Dinmont Terrier Club and are largely responsible for the open culture of knowledge sharing – freely given, nurtured and passed on – which ensures that the Dandie is not only preserved, but cherished. "These dogs are too important to let go, and there are lots of us working hard for them. It is great to see new and young folk finding out what great family dogs they are," Ali says with a smile as Morty nudges her hand, telling her not to stop scrunching his ears.

In the hands of these keepers of the flame, our doggy heritage burns steady and bright. They don't ask for applause. But here's a toast to the lassies – for their grit, their laughter and the sacred work they do keeping Scotland's beloved dogs safe, sound and ready to chum generations yet to come. Slàinte mhath!

THE LITTLEST LAIRD

The Border Terrier

BREED STANDARD

GENERAL APPEARANCE: Small, hardy and built for work with an otter-like head.
COAT: Harsh, dense outer coat with a short, soft undercoat.
COLOUR: Red, grizzle and tan, blue and tan, or wheaten.
EYES: Dark with a keen expression.
MOVEMENT: Narrow-bodied with sound, ground-covering movement.
TEMPERAMENT: Alert, affectionate and game for anything.

A RUGGED RASCAL

Small, scruffy and spirited – the Border terrier carries the hardy soul of the Border country between Scotland and England in its wiry coat. With an otter-like face, dark keen eyes and a body superbly built for endurance and earth-work, they might trot past you in a village in Roxburghshire or Northumberland and not turn heads like a fancy show dog, but spend a day in the hills with one and you'll see why farmers and families alike have adored them for generations. They are unassuming but bold, affectionate yet independent, and their personalities really are the perfect mix of cockiness and scallywag. One second a Border terrier is curled up having a snooze on your lap, the next they're streaking after a rabbit with single-minded zeal.

Even in the harsh winds of the Cheviot Hills, the Border terrier keeps pace. They were bred to run with the pack – quite literally – and this heritage shows in their long-legged stride and tireless gait. But if you meet a Border in a home setting, you're just as likely to be greeted with a paw and a warm lean against your leg. This is a breed that doesn't put on airs. Sturdy of body and modest in size, the Border terrier seems content to let its deeds do the talking. They are capable wee rascals: down to earth, lively and communicative.

GENTLE AT HOME, FIERCE IN THE FIELD

Beneath the Border's shaggy eyebrows and mild expression lies a personality as big and bold as that of a dog ten times its size. They love human company and tend not to be as quarrelsome towards other dogs as some of their terrier cousins.

They are loyal without being clingy, content to relax at your feet after a good pootle round the village. But when duty calls – from the moment they pick up the scent of cats, squirrels or rabbits – that old fire ignites. Being born of generations of terriers bred to chase foxes and exterminate vermin has wired them to respond instantly to movement. They tend to wake early and love routine, but boredom can be the enemy of any terrier, and if a Border isn't getting enough exercise and interaction, a fenced garden will become an excavation site or a kitchen chair might be subject to a sudden makeover with gnawing teeth.

Still, living with a Border is a joy. Many owners speak of their Border's almost human-like understanding – that tilt of the head and knowing look when you talk to them. They can be sensitive to their people's moods: a Border will often stick close by if you're feeling under the weather, offering empathetic companionship. While not as cuddly as some breeds, most Borders are affectionate in

GROUP: Terrier.
STATUS: Secure.
ORIGIN: Evolving in the border region between Scotland and England, the Border terrier was bred in the early 1800s to work alongside foxhounds, bolting foxes that had gone to ground.
HEIGHT: 25–28 cm.
WEIGHT: Male: 6–7 kg. Female: 5–6.5 kg.

Socialisation
Friendliness
Trainability

Size

Colour

The Border Terrier

their own way – nudging their shoulder into you for a pat or napping with their chin resting on your foot.

Their terse coat does just the trick in any weather Scotland can throw at them, and this bristly cloak is so characteristic of the breed – slowly wearing in like a comfy tweed jacket – with grey whiskers gradually appearing as they mature. They are one of the breeds that don't seem to need a bath quite so often, never really carrying that musty doggy smell, and they are more or less self-cleaning in the rain.

FORGED IN THE BORDER HILLS

To understand this terrier, we need to head out to the rolling borderlands of Scotland and England, and the work that farmers and shepherds have done there for centuries. In these hills, foxes were a constant menace to livestock, and the locals needed a dog that could pursue any den dweller and chase them out into the open. In the eighteenth century, a distinct type of terrier began to emerge – neither prim nor fancy, they were bred for the tenacity that fox-adverse farmers required. At first, folk referred to them by the names of the different valleys in Northumberland where they were revered as trusty tykes that could get the job done.

DID YOU KNOW?
BITE-SIZED BORDER

- **Origins:** These dogs were originally known as Coquetdale or Redesdale terriers, reflecting their emergence in Northumberland breeding grounds.
- **What's in a Name?:** The term Border terrier was first popularised around 1880 thanks to the breed's long association with the Border Hunt. The hunt's masters, John Robson and John Dodd, bred such renowned terriers that their dogs were soon simply called Border terriers, solidifying the breed's name.
- **First of the Line:** In 1913, The Moss Trooper became the first Border terrier to be registered with the British Kennel Club. Bred by Jacob Robson, John's grandson, from his trusted working dogs, he was entered before the breed even had its own official classification.

A' mire ri cuilein, cha sgur e gus an sgal e.
Playing with a pup (or a child) ends in a howl.

> **DID YOU KNOW?**
> **BITE-SIZED BORDER**
> - **Celebrity Owners:** The Border terrier's fan club includes Andy Murray, Scotland's tennis hero, who had two Borders, Maggie May and Rusty. Maggie May famously authored a tongue-in-cheek Twitter account with updates on Andy's matches.
> - **The Dug That Didn't Bark:** Unlike many terriers, the Border was prized for his silence in the field; a good working dog would trail a scent and bolt a fox without a sound.
> - **Houdini or Hound?** Don't let that scruffy innocence fool you. Borders are famous escape artists – they can scale surprisingly high fences or dig under them with determined speed.

By the mid-1800s, organised fox hunting was in full swing among the British gentry, and these hunts took note of the tough little terriers and their vermin control skills. A pivotal moment came in 1857, when John Robson and John Dodd, two country gentlemen and avid huntsmen, founded the Border Hunt in Northumberland. It's easy to imagine that landowners and sporting types from neighbouring counties – Durham, Cumbria, Berwickshire and Midlothian – would have taken a keen interest, not wanting to miss the establishment of a new hunt in such promising landscapes. Alongside foxhounds, packs of local working terriers were maintained – these dogs were fast enough to keep pace with horses, yet small and game enough for the task, too.

Among the hunt staff were the terriermen. Working-class men, not part of the mounted field and not dressed for show, they were there to assist and to follow the action with their own pack. When a fox went to ground, it was their job to step in with the tenacious terriers who specialised in flushing out the fox from where the barking hounds could not go. Once within a fox's den, the terriers worked in silence and darkness, relying on their instincts and digging where necessary.

In time, their usefulness and stamina drew admiration from hunting circles well beyond the Borders, and word of their merits travelled far. I imagine that visitors to the hunt from, as it were, out of town would take dogs away with them – thus spreading the fame and increasing the presence of these wiry rough-coated terriers across the country.

FROM FOX DEN TO FAMILY FRIEND

On 24 June 1920, at a meeting held in the town of Hawick in the Scottish Borders, the Border Terrier Club was established. At last, the Border terrier was on an equal footing with other dogs of the day and included in the culture of formalisation. Robson and Dodd were there to draft the first official breed standard, which perfectly described the region's small, sought-after dog. They paid special attention to the head – insisting it must be shaped like that of an otter – evoking it as strong-jawed but not overly long, to allow the dog to grip its prey and still manoeuvre in tight burrows.

Over time, the breed's endearing qualities were noticed in wider circles, and by the mid-twentieth century, the once obscure Border terrier was quietly moving indoors, onto comfortable knees and rugs in front of fires. Scottish and English families discovered what a lovely house dog a Border could make – affectionate, trainable and full of fun. The

breed soon had a wee foot in two worlds; it could patrol the barn for vermin by day and receive cuddles from the children of a family when it relaxed in the evening after a busy 9-to-5 of pest control!

One figure who came to appreciate this adaptability was James Herriot, the Yorkshire veterinarian and author of *All Creatures Great and Small*. After a lifetime treating other people's animals, Herriot finally got a Border terrier of his own in retirement, and he named him Bodie. Herriot was utterly smitten with this little guy and would later write, "No dog has ever given me so much joy as Bodie." Herriot, who had tended everything from Great Danes to farmyard collies, and lived with many breeds, too, found the perfect companion for his old age in this scruffy terrier, adroit stealer of the veteran vet's heart!

A Border terrier even made it onto a postage stamp in America, or so the story goes. In the late nineteenth century, a shaggy little terrier wandered into the post office in Albany, New York. No one knew where he'd come from, but the postal clerks took a shine to him. The dog, soon named Owney, began riding the railway mail trains, curling up on sacks of post as they chugged and rattled across the country.

Over time, Owney became something of a celebrity, and railway workers considered him a good-luck charm. As his adventures grew, clerks began attaching tags to his collar to record his journeys, and eventually he had so many that the Postmaster General commissioned a special harness to carry them all. In total, he reportedly travelled more than 140,000 miles back and forth across the United States.

In 2011, more than a century after his final journey, a US postage stamp commemorated Owney, medals and all. Today, his tag collection is on display at the Smithsonian National Postal Museum in Washington, DC. While his exact breed is unknown, Owney is widely thought to have been a type of Border terrier or terrier mix, and, judging by the photographs, it's easy to see why.

A BORDERLINE CULTURAL ICON IN MINIATURE

In recent years, the Border terrier has often ranked among the most popular breeds registered with the Kennel Club. City dwellers and country folk alike have discovered that they are a joy to live with whether in a rural setting or amid city streets.

Though, technically, a Border breed straddling two nations, the Border terrier is deeply entwined with Scottish life. To share your time with a Border terrier is to have a scrap of Scottish Borders history curled up at your feet, even if "the hunt" now thankfully means a romp in the park after a ball or a stick. Above all, a Border in your home means knowing that the spirit of the Borders – resilient, generous and a tad wild and windswept – lives on in a wee dog with a very braw heart.

THE KILCHRENAN TRIO

If you head down to the loch today, you're sure to get a surprise – noses down, tails high and a blur of bracken-charging Border terriers living their best lives. Meet Isbean, Sgadan and Jock: three characters in one family, a trio who are the life and soul of the household.

Life is never dull with three Border terriers in tow, and Ceitidh and Cameron are famous in their village of Kilchrenan because of this loveable pack of bristly champs. The eldest of them, the matriarch, is Isbean – she's four and was named by Ceitidh with a healthy dose of mischief. Isbean means sausage in Gaelic, which has led to more than a few pub-side chuckles and more than one confused receptionist at the vet's office. But there's a method to the moniker! "I wanted Gaelic names that were a bit playful," says Ceitidh. "And once you've got a sausage, you might as well have a herring too." Hence Sgadan, a pup named for the silver darlings. Last of all came Jock – a fine, firm-footed Scottish favourite and the name chosen by Cameron.

Ceitidh didn't grow up with dogs, but longed for one all her life. Cameron, by contrast, was raised on a farm surrounded by working collies and terriers. When the time was right, they set out to find a small dog that could keep pace with their outdoor lifestyle and, after much research, they decided upon the Border terrier. Enter Isbean, who arrived as a bundle of wiry fuzz with a beard "like a miniature sage".

Breeding had never been part of the plan, but as Isbean grew, it became clear she had something special. After months of preparation, she delivered a litter of seven, and Ceitidh was right there beside her. "I was bursting with pride," she says. "She trusted me entirely. It felt like a silent bond had been formed in that moment." They had only meant to keep one pup, but Sgadan won Ceitidh's heart, and Jock, with his belly-up ways and puppy-eyed charm, had comprehensively secured Cameron's. "We talked and we debated . . . and eventually we admitted we weren't letting either of them go."

Though they share the same bloodline, the personalities of the three dogs couldn't be more different. Isbean is undisputed queen of the house – headstrong, selective with her affections and a tyke on the terrier-racing circuit. "She once won three shows in a row," Ceitidh says with a proud grin. But don't be fooled. If the weather turns wet, she's a duvet-dweller of the highest order. One damp day, or so I was told, she refused to leave the bed until mid-afternoon!

Sgadan is the rebel. First to scale the puppy pen like it was built for climbing practice and most likely to launch himself into the middle of a cèilidh, he's a real crowd pleaser. He's a loyal soul once he knows you, but until then, he keeps his cards close. Food is his love language, and he's got a glint in his eye that spells trouble and fun in equal measure.

Then there's Jock, a cuddle merchant like no other. "If I hadn't seen him be born, I'd swear he was a different breed," laughs Ceitidh. He shimmies on his back for belly rubs, lets himself be cradled like a baby and would happily trade treats for affection any day of the week. This wee fellow is the heart of the pack.

Together they've reshaped daily life. They certainly get Ceitidh out in the hills, following their noses to new places, snuffling through heather and chasing the wind. "We do scavenger hunts and breed-fulfilment games – it's brilliant." And somehow, despite the madness, life fits together like it was meant to be, for everyone. Even the cat, Hector, has carved out his place as the undisputed feline boss of the household.

"They're small scruffs with mighty personalities," says Ceitidh, "not to be underestimated at any cost." In a world of polished breeds and prim pedigrees, the Border terrier remains gloriously itself. Brave, bold, a bit daft and endlessly devoted. Much like this riotous wee trio of Border terrier brand ambassadors from Kilchrenan.

BLACK AND FLAME

The Gordon Setter

BREED STANDARD

GENERAL APPEARANCE: Stylish, noble, substantial and symmetrical with plenty of bone and muscle, built for stamina over speed.
COAT: Soft, straight or slightly wavy – feathered on ears, chest, legs and tail.
COLOUR: Black with clearly defined, rich chestnut or mahogany markings on muzzle, chest, legs and under-tail.
EYES: Dark brown, bright and intelligent, neither deep-set nor prominent.
MOVEMENT: Free-flowing and ground-covering with strong drive from the hindquarters.
TEMPERAMENT: Alert, confident, affectionate, bold and self-assured.

SCOTLAND'S SETTER

A Gordon setter's silken coat ripples and glints in dappled light; black as night, it flickers with chestnut-hued fires. As if to highlight such canine elegance, it moves with an effortless precision. The Gordon setter doesn't bound – its feathered ears and tail flow in exact synchronicity with its breathtaking motion. This is no frantic dog, no scattergun scout. It might be a touch daft at times, but the Gordon setter will earnestly hold your gaze and is, unmistakably, a noble hunter with presence.

Bred at Gordon Castle in Moray, this marvelous Scottish gundog has been shaped by centuries of fieldcraft and was never meant to vanish into the background. And yet, to our loss, it has. Once a familiar sight on Highland shoots, the Gordon setter has slipped into rarity. But for those who know – who have walked behind one as it locks to an outlined point against the moor – there's no doubt that this is one of Scotland's finest gifts to the world of working dogs.

CHARACTER & COMPANIONSHIP

The Gordon setter is a magnificent dog, with a (mostly) angelic nature. Affectionate – some might say devoted – they nevertheless retain a strong independent streak. This is a breed with opinions; they are intelligent, sensitive and sometimes stubborn. They thrive best with an experienced owner who understands how to pitch the perfect balance of firm guidance and gentle encouragement.

There's a dignity to the Gordon setter; as if shaped by weather and distance, they have a timeless depth about them. They don't greet strangers with wagging exuberance, but they don't bristle either: they simply hold their space, calmly, until the room makes sense to them. For those they trust, the bond runs deep – but for these dogs, it's more about belonging than approval. If they follow you, it's not from need, but from choice. If they watch you, it's with stillness and observation, not demand. This is a dog that prefers silence to noise, purpose to pampering, and offers an appreciative, non-declarative loyalty.

As with most dogs, early socialisation is key. Gordons can be wary, and if not introduced to new people, dogs and environments during their formative months, they may grow cautious or reactive. But with the right start, they will bloom into confident, composed companions.

Their training requires a deft hand, preferably that of an expert. Gordons are not robotic obedience dogs – they must believe in the reason behind any task before they'll give it their all. Forceful

GROUP: Gundog.
STATUS: Vulnerable.
ORIGIN: Developed at Gordon Castle in Morayshire, this beautiful and distinctive setter was bred to be a versatile, elegant hunting dog for Highland game.
HEIGHT: Male: 66 cm. Female: 62 cm
WEIGHT: Male: 29.5 kg. Female: 25.5 kg.

methods are counterproductive (as they are with all dogs, of course); these dogs respond best to consistency of tone and mutual trust. Once the bond is formed, a Gordon will work with quiet precision, even in the most challenging terrain.

BLACK & TAN BEAUTY

The Gordon's coat is one of its defining, most striking features: a rich black with clearly defined mahogany or chestnut markings on the muzzle, chest, legs and beneath the tail. The feathering on the ears, chest, legs and tail gives a luxurious look, almost like that of velvet drape.

Grooming is moderate but consistent. Weekly brushing is required to prevent mats, particularly behind the ears and along the distinctive feathering, and regular checks for bramble thorns after long walks are essential. Their ears are prone to wax build-up, so cleaning around those fantastic lugs should be part of the routine. Indoors, they are relatively clean dogs, but do love a good mud wallow when the mood strikes – particularly after a swim or a gallop through the bracken.

HEALTH & LONGEVITY

Bred to be hardy and tireless in the field, Gordon setters are generally robust and athletic, with a typical lifespan of ten to twelve years. But, like many pedigree

---

DID YOU KNOW? GORDON SETTER TRIVIA

- **The Castle Dog:** Gordon setters were once nicknamed "castle dogs" due to their strong association with the Duke of Gordon's estate at Gordon Castle. These dogs were so highly prized that a good one was said to be "worth more than a horse in full condition". In a twist on the famous saying, a racehorse becomes a poor man's Gordon setter!
- **Black & Tan by Design:** The Gordon's iconic black-and-tan colouring was a deliberate choice. The Duke of Gordon favoured this darker coat to help distinguish his dogs from the paler English setters of the time.
- **Steadier Than Most:** Compared to other setters, Gordons have a reputation for being the "steadiest" on point – a trait valued on Highland moors where birds were sparse and every opportunity mattered.

> **Na biodh gun chù, 's na beathaich cuilean.**
> *Don't be without a dog, but don't rear a pup.*

dogs and you'll soon discover that a bored Gordon is rarely a quiet one! They need space to roam, puzzles to solve, scents to track and routines that give genuine purpose. Long moorland walks, scent games in the garden and a good lope through safe countryside are all regular features on the Gordon's to-do list.

In the right environment, they are not just active, they are fulfilled. And when a Gordon setter is fulfilled, it becomes one of the most dignified, rewarding companions a dog lover could ask for.

A HIGHLAND INHERITANCE

The Gordon setter takes its name from Alexander, 4th Duke of Gordon, a Highland aristocrat affectionately known as the "Cock of the North". More than a titled landowner, the duke was a builder of regiments, villages and legacies. He raised the famed Gordon Highlanders in 1794, an infantry regiment drawn from the northeast that would go on to earn distinction in battlefields across the world. He redeveloped the village of Fochabers as a model community, shaped by Enlightenment ideals, and he expanded Gordon Castle into one of Scotland's grandest homes. He also championed Scottish traditional arts, acting as patron to the composer and fiddler William Marshall – his estate steward and one of Scotland's finest writers of strathspeys

breeds, they carry the potential for certain inherited conditions. Among the most common are hip dysplasia, progressive retinal atrophy, hypothyroidism and gastric torsion (bloat) – a serious and potentially life-threatening condition that demands immediate veterinary care. Responsible breeders screen for these issues, so don't be shy in seeking assurances.

The Gordon's vitality is what makes it such a charmer, but it also presents a real challenge. As a breed, they thrive on movement and mental stimulation. Denied an outlet, the Gordon becomes restless – vocal, frustrated and possibly destructive. Spend any time with these

and reels who composed over two hundred tunes.

But of all the duke's lasting contributions, perhaps none are more enduring than the dog that bears his name. At Gordon Castle, he gathered and refined a line of black and tan setters, favouring a steady, intelligent working style above all else. These dogs were recognisable, infamous even – heavier boned, slower paced and with a silhouette evoking a certain Highland elegance. They were bred to range across rough moorland and cover terrain where a dog of substance and stamina was prized. Alexander favoured the then unusual tan and black colouring as opposed to the flashier white and orange English setters of the day.

After the duke's death in 1827, the breed's development continued with fanciers across Scotland and England. For a time, it was known as the "black and tan setter", but the snappier name of "Gordon setter" was the one that stuck. The Kennel Club officially recognised the breed in 1872, and it quickly gained a following on both sides of the Atlantic. Today, despite their heritage, Gordon setters are far less common than their gundog cousins. Sadly, in 2024, the Kennel Club of the UK once again listed them as a vulnerable native breed.

DID YOU KNOW? GORDON SETTER TRIVIA

- **An American Favourite:** Gordon setters were among the first breeds recognised by the American Kennel Club founded in 1884. They appear in the 1887 Stud Book and, for a time, enjoyed greater popularity across the Atlantic than in their native Scotland.
- **A Dog of Two Worlds:** In the Victorian era, Gordons were praised as "gentleman's companions". These beautiful dogs were stylish enough for society and rugged enough for the hills.
- **The Slow Burner:** Gordons are famously slow to mature, often taking up to three years to fully come into their own.
- **Highland DNA:** Genetic studies confirm the Gordon setter's close relationship to other setters, though its roots remain firmly tied to the Highlands.

THE NOBLE WORKER

As a gundog, the Gordon setter was bred for stamina and discernment: frankly, they are designed for a long day of work. Known for being a methodical searcher rather than a zigzagging sprinter, the setter's style is measured. It covers ground in a purposeful quartering pattern with head held high, reading the wind, analysing scent and conserving energy for what could be hours of effort. One might say it's an approach mirroring that of a hardy endurance runner seeking a path through the hills.

Gordon setters are natural pointers, instinctively freezing the instant they locate game. In these statuesque moments, they seem to defy the laws of motion, and it's this steadiness that defines them. Some breeds excel at covering a wideness of ground, but Gordons excel at holding point often for minutes at a time. On the hill, where birds may be few and the ground tough, that determination becomes an extraordinary virtue – a rushed flush might squander the only shot of the day.

This trait made them ideal for traditional Highland sport, where walking guns and keepers relied on a dog that wouldn't break early or over-run scent. A well-schooled Gordon could track a grouse's movement across shifting winds, adapt to the land and stay fixed to its task even in the foulest of weather. They gained a reputation for memory, too – able to recall scenting grounds, dips and dells from previous outings, building a mental map of the moor with uncanny precision and intelligence.

Though less frequently used in the shooting field today, the Gordon's skills have proven transferable. They adapt well to advanced scent work, tracking and working trials, and their calm, intuitive nature makes them increasingly popular as therapy dogs. In every setting, what endures is their focus, their patience and their understated brilliance. (Oh and their debonair good looks!)

GLOBAL REACH & BREED CONSERVATION

Although rooted in the Scottish Highlands, the Gordon setter's style and steadiness have earned it admirers worldwide. In the United States, they were recognised by the American Kennel Club as early as 1884 and have developed strong working and show lines across the continent. In Scandinavia, Gordons are favoured as reliable field dogs in the Nordic terrain, where their slower pace and stamina are well appreciated.

Back home, numbers have dwindled, but breed clubs and conservationists are working to raise awareness of these Caledonian canines. They are a living reminder of Scotland's heritage, deserving of protection and celebration for generations to come. The Gordon Setter Club of Scotland and like-minded groups promote responsible breeding, support working trials and encourage new admirers to discover the sheer classiness of the breed. In the right household, when they turn up to share your life, they ultimately complete it.

THE CLOHASS GORDON SETTERS

It all started with a promise to herself. Christine was just a girl when she first laid eyes on a setter – an Irish one, working the fields on her grandmother's land. Tall, lean and red as flame, the dog moved with such elegance and grace that she silently vowed, "One day, I'll have a setter of my own."

That day came fifty-five years ago, with Ruagh the Irish setter, but it was a chance encounter in an Oban pub that changed everything. "I saw a Gordon setter sitting there – absolutely stunning – and I was hooked."

For the last three decades, Christine has shared her life with Gordons – gloriously loyal, loving and full of intent. Her first was Isla, followed by Cara, then Staffa – each one a chapter in a story that now stretches across generations. Today, her four girls – Fidra, Shian, Luing and Nave – all carry those lines forward, descended from the very first Clohass dogs, and yes they are named for Scottish islands. They are her constant companions, confidantes and entertainers. It would be fair to say that they are, 100 per cent, family.

Fidra (Clohass Leezie Lindsay), now nearly fourteen, is the grande dame of the household. Most of her day is spent "sofa surfing" between the lounge and the conservatory, but if you dare try to leave the house without her, you'll be swiftly corrected. "Not on your nelly," Christine laughs.

Shian (Clohass Caol Ila), seven and a half, is the household clock. She announces walk time, dinner time and bedtime too, with unwavering certainty. There's no need for alarms or schedules – Shian will keep you on track for every important appointment.

Then there's Luing (Clohass Black Lace), age six and a half – elegant, composed and just a touch superior. "She's the princess," says Christine. "She looks down her nose like she's a cut above the rest." She's also the most prolific talker. Gordon setters, Christine says, are great conversationalists – and Luing leads the chorus. "She woos and yodels at you, full on back and forth. It's like having a chat with a feathery soprano."

And finally, there's Nave (Clohass Ardmaddy), the youngest at a year and a half, and the only one still being shown. She's affectionately known as the Artful Dodger – a tissue thief, a pocket-picker and an energetic blur of chaos. "She loves pinching things and running for the hills with them," Christine says with a grin. "We call her Kangaroo – she bounces everywhere."

When it comes to the show ring, Nave can be sublime – or silly. "She'll

either show beautifully or decide it's just a lovely day out and bounce round the ring like she's at a party." Still, she's no slouch. Nave has qualified for Crufts two years running and is clearly more than capable of holding her own in strong company.

The Gordon setter, Christine says, is a breed genuinely apart. It's sensitive to your feelings, affectionate and full of personality. They thrive on movement, muddy woods and a big cosy couch to crash on at the end of the day. "They think they're lap dogs," she says with a big shrug. "They'll climb up and wrap themselves around your neck like a scarf."

Over the years, the dogs have brought more than canine exuberance – they've brought people. "I've made so many friends through showing. We've shared meals, memories, pedigrees – and many a happy hour chatting about dogs long gone." She remembers the emotion of her first litter, the awe of each new pup arriving and the thrill of making up Staffa as her first show champion. One unforgettable moment was doing the double – winning both Challenge Certificates, dog and bitch, at the same show.

Now, with her four girls around her, Christine sees generations layered into each other – habits, expressions and quirks passed down like heirlooms. "You see little bits of the parents, the grandparents, even the great-grandparents. They're all in there." For Christine, there's nothing better than being there to witness her setters stretch out through the forest, galloping full-pelt, ears flying and eyes shining. It's a joy that never fades. "I just love watching them enjoy themselves. They're part of the family, every one of them."

Christine would be the last person to boast, but those who know the breed know her name. With pups across continents, Clohass Gordon setters have gone far and wide – bringing joy, companionship and extraordinary standards of quality to families and breeders alike. She has played a quiet, vital role in preserving the breed's future, one carefully planned pairing and adoringly raised litter at a time.

But like all the best breeders, Christine is a dog lover first and foremost: her girls mean far more to her than their pedigrees or show results. Her Gordon setters are velvety-pawed house dwellers, walk buddies and beloved individuals. And perhaps her best advocacy for the breed shines most brightly in the fact that both her children live with gorgeous Gordons: Jonathan has Parker, and Kirsten with partner James has Anam – and thus it is that the legacy of the Clohass kennel looks set to continue for many years to come.

A SHAGGY SHEPHERD

The Bearded Collie

BREED STANDARD

GENERAL APPEARANCE: Medium-sized, lean, active and well-balanced with a bright, alert expression.
COAT: Double coat with soft undercoat and flat, harsh, shaggy outer coat.
COLOUR: Slate grey, reddish fawn, black, blue, all with or without white markings.
EYES: Toned to coat colour, large and set wide apart.
MOVEMENT: Smooth, supple, ground-covering trot with strong drive.
TEMPERAMENT: Alert, lively, self-confident and affectionate.

TANGLES & LOYALTY

The bearded collie is a bounding bundle of energy and affection, a shaggy-haired herder with a twinkle in its eye. With its trademark beard, tousled coat and ever-wagging tail, the Beardie is one of Scotland's most beloved working breeds. Developed in the Highlands for driving cattle and sheep across vast expanses of rugged terrain, it earned its reputation – and its place within the working life of the country – through stamina, wit and willpower as the most competent of drovers. Their talent for independent decision-making often rivals that of their collie cousins – and that's saying something, given how savvy collies are.

Under their ebullient weatherproof coats is a dog of substance – athletic, clever and fiercely tenacious. The bearded collie eked out an important role in rural Scottish life as a tireless worker. And at home, a Beardie makes for a loyal and watchful companion, who is often the liveliest soul in the room.

BRAINS UNDER THE BEARD

Talk with anyone who's lived with a Beardie about the breed and chances are they'll break into a grin. Famed for their joyful, affectionate nature, it's easy to see why people fall for them. But for all the cuteness of their flowing locks, it's their intelligence that really stands out.

Bearded collies are super smart, resourceful and confident dogs. Bred to work independently, they developed a keen mind of their own. They learn quickly, but also absolutely think for themselves. Training a Beardie can feel like negotiating with a clever toddler – and, of course, toddlers and dogs alike tend to respond best to positive, fun methods, whereas rigidity or unnecessary strictness can bring out their wilful side.

Their owners will often tell stories of the Beardie sense of humour. These dogs know how to make you laugh, racing through a big mucky puddle at the worst possible time or tilting their head just so, as if in on the joke. They are high spirited, but gentle at heart; a well-socialised Beardie is friendly with people and usually good with other animals. They may give a hearty bark when someone comes to the door, but moments later you'll be greeted by that trademark grin. In essence, a Beardie is a shaggy, cheery extrovert full of affection and glee.

BRUSHING UP ON BEARDIES

It would be foolish to pretend otherwise . . . keeping a bearded collie means welcoming a bit of the outdoors indoors. That luxurious coat will bring in sand from the beach, burrs from the field and enough stoor to pattern your floors on a rainy day. Grooming is a serious

GROUP: Pastoral.
STATUS: Vulnerable.
ORIGIN: Bred by Scottish shepherds, the Bearded collie was developed to herd livestock with independence and over long distance across rugged terrain.
HEIGHT: Male: 53–56 cm. Female: 51–53 cm
WEIGHT: Male: 20.5–27 kg. Female: 16–23 kg.

Socialisation: 4/5
Friendliness: 5/5
Trainability: 4/5

commitment; the ideal is daily brushing or combing to prevent tangles and matting. Many owners establish a comfortable evening routine with the dog stretched out on the rug and the human armed with a brush, working through the long fur while recounting the day's events to a pair of patient, attentive eyes. Come the autumn or spring shedding seasons, one might joke that a Beardie could knit you another dog with the amount of fur it drops. Yet, with regular care, that truly magnificent coat is manageable.

These are active dogs that were bred to trot miles every day behind stock, so a walk around the block, however brisk, won't satisfy them. They really need a good hour or more of daily exercise. Mental stimulation is just as important: a bored Beardie might decide to reorganise your household (chewing a shoe here, herding a posse of small children there), but given a job or activity, they'll throw themselves into it with gusto. It speaks to the breed's versatility that a dog who once expertly herded sheep on a hillside can adapt to urban family life as long as its mind and body are kept active.

Bearded collies are deeply social. They thrive on company and connection, and you will often find them shadowing owners, happy to simply be near their human companions. Sensitive and intuitive, they'll nudge your hand when they

> **DID YOU KNOW? BEARDED COLLIE CURIOSITIES**
> - **What's in a Name?:** The bearded collie's many nicknames tell a story; besides Beardie, they've been called Highland collies and Muir collies, and in old Scots, the hairy mou'ed (hairy-mouthed) collie– a perfect description of their fuzzy muzzle.
> - **A 500-Year Legacy:** Folk tradition says a Polish trader brought Polish Lowland sheepdogs to Scotland in 1514, and that these may have helped to create the Beardie.
> - **The Accidental Ancestor:** Almost all modern bearded collies trace their lineage back to a single wartime pup called Jeannie, who was sent to her owner by mistake during a postal mix-up.

> **DID YOU KNOW? BEARDED COLLIE CURIOSITIES**
>
> - **Coat of Many Colours:** Bearded collie puppies are born in one of four basic colours – black, brown, blue or fawn – but they often pale dramatically during their first year, sometimes becoming silvery or slate-grey. The breed standard recognises seventeen official colour combinations, including various shades with white or tricolour markings.
> - **The Beardie Bounce:** That famous joyful leap isn't just for play. Many Beardies bounce up on their hind legs to greet you, a habit that echoes their heritage as agile, intuitive herders. In the working hills, they would spring above the bracken to spot sheep or signal their position across rough terrain.

sense you're feeling low, or bounce into a playful act if they think the moment might merit a laugh. They genuinely seem to want to live life by your side – emotionally and physically.

THE HAIRY HERDER

Like many old Scottish breeds, the bearded collie's origins mix fact with a dash of legend – one oft-repeated tale traces their lineage to sheepdogs from Poland, brought to Scotland in the early 1500s by a grain merchant from Gdańsk. He had travelled to the Borders to purchase sheep and brought along his Polish Lowland sheepdogs to manage the flock. Local shepherds were so impressed that they traded sheep in exchange for a few of the dogs. These were then bred with native Scottish working stock – and from that cross came the early bearded collie type.

We will probably never know whether or not the blood of those Polish sheepdogs courses through their veins, but there have been skilled herding dogs in Scotland for centuries who earned their keep driving stock to market towns. In his 1891 book *The Dogs of Scotland*, D. J. Thomson Gray paints a vivid – if rather blunt – portrait of the bearded collie, describing it as "a big, rough, 'tousy' tyke with a coat not unlike a doormat", its hair is "hard and fibry", and its ears hang close to the head. While the comparison may seem unkind, these words capture a practical truth: that shaggy, unkempt coat was a vital tool not a superficial accident. Coarse and weatherproof, it shielded the Beardie from rain, snow and biting wind, allowing it to work for hours in Scotland's all-too-familiar wild elements.

By the early twentieth century, however, the Beardie nearly faded into history as their role was increasingly taken up by their slicker-coated, easier-managed kin in the collie group. The Second World War and changing postwar times led to a mere handful of Beardies left in Scotland; it's said only four were registered over the eight years from 1939 to 1948: the breed was on the brink of extinction.

JEANNIE OF BOTHKENNAR

Salvation came in the form of a happy accident and a determined woman. In 1944, a Scottish farmer sent Mrs G. Olive Willison a dog she had requested for her kennel. She had asked for a Shetland sheepdog, but what tumbled out of the crate was no dainty Sheltie! Here was a gangly, floppy-eared scrap of a dog with a shaggy coat and mischief in every step – a bearded collie.

So she had been sent the wrong breed, but rather than send the pup back, Mrs Willison became enchanted with her new girl. She named her Jeannie and thus was set in motion one of the greatest comeback stories in dogdom. Mrs Willison sought a mate for her unexpected Beardie, and in a chance meeting on a beach in Sussex, she encountered a Scotsman who needed a home for his grey bearded collie. Sensing another serendipitous opportunity, she took in the sturdy fellow, registered him as Bailie of Bothkennar and introduced him to Jeannie. The rest, as they say, is history.

In 1947, the pair produced a litter of puppies that would become the foundation of the modern bearded collie breed. From Jeannie and Bailie sprang the line of Bothkennar Beardies, ensuring that the ancient shaggy dogs of Scotland would not be lost after all. Other enthusiasts joined the effort, scouring the country for any remaining Beardies of sound working stock. Notably, a blue-grey working collie named Turnbull's Blue, owned by a Scottish shepherd, was brought into the breeding activity, adding genetic depth to the revived lines.

A new Bearded Collie Club was formed in 1955, and the Kennel Club

HALF-BROTHER COLLIES OF THE HILL

Every morning, come rain or shine, two familiar figures appear on our croft beside the Cromore fold. They are Mac and Jeff, half-brother collies with Border blood and a dash of Beardie bounce. Their bond with Tanya, their owner, is clear in every stride – they herd sheep, chase balls and share a daily nose kiss with the Highland cows; the latter being a ritual of understanding between the species that is pure instinct. To see even a trace of Beardie blood alive in local working lines is a joy. In Mac and Jeff, tradition lives on in the intelligence in their eyes and the wispy traces of their fur.

THE TRAVELLERS' LEGACY

Though the bearded collie has no single ancestral home, its survival owes much to informal expertise – in the centuries before formal breeding and Kennel Club standards, Beardie pups were passed from croft to croft, or traded at the mart. And some of the most significant, unsung guardians of these bloodlines were Scotland's Traveller families.

Scottish Traveller and storyteller Jess Smith recalls how her father, Charles Riley, would journey across the land with his favourite fox terrier, Tiny. He'd stop at farms and estates, offering to clear the

officially recognised the breed in 1959. In just over a decade, the Beardie went from rarity to revival – a truly impressive resurrection from near oblivion. Willison remained closely involved with the breed's development until her death. The story began with a simple mistake and a chance meeting, but Olive never sought credit or fame – only to preserve the dog she had grown to love.

vermin from sheds and byres, thereby setting the place right with his Tiny workforce for the season ahead, in exchange for a few shillings and hospitality for the day. "He had a way with dogs," Jess told me, "and the dogs had a way with him."

That way runs deep in the Traveller tradition. Dogs were companions, workers and protectors – and, often, they created a bridge between Traveller and settled folk. It's easy to imagine that just as they brought skills, songs and stories from one glen to the next, Traveller families also carried working bloodlines across Scotland. A Beardie pup picked up in Pitlochry might end up in Peebles, bartered for a new harness, oil for the lamp or a pair of sturdy boots. These exchanges kept the lines fresh and varied, the instincts sharp and, ultimately, the breed alive – not through paperwork or pedigree, but through people who knew the worth of a good dog.

And so this was a different kind of breeding. It wasn't driven by conformation or show ribbons, but by need, trust and a whole host of practical skills. In short, the people of the Traveller communities knew a fine dog when they saw one. The dogs they chose, and bred, could think, guard, herd and were a form of valuable currency.

As rural Scotland began to change after the Second World War – with, for example, new farming systems and the slow erosion of the travelling way of life – the networks of dogs changing hands faded too. But it's worth remembering that for generations, Travellers were the living, foundational lifeline that ensured working breeds were protected and that remote farms never went without a decent dog.

WHY THE BEARDIE MATTERS

Today, the bearded collie is adored around the world and it remains a particularly beloved part of Scotland's canine heritage. You might still spot a few working Beardies on farms, but more commonly they shine now as therapy dogs – their gentle, biddable nature brings comfort in care homes and hospitals – or as the all-stars of obedience and agility trials.

In 1989, a bearded collie named Potterdale Classic of Moonhill – known to friends as Cassie – stepped into the ring at Crufts and into the history books. Bred and owned by Brenda White, Cassie became the first, and only, Beardie to win Best in Show at Britain's most prestigious dog show. With her flowing coat and unmistakable bounce, she showed that a scruffy hill dog could hold its own among the world's most polished pooches and win an enthusiastic, discerning crowd over to boot.

Despite moments of fame, the bearded collie's fortunes have ebbed and flowed. In recent years, it's been added to the Kennel Club's list of vulnerable native breeds – a reminder that even the most beloved dogs can slip from view. So why does the Beardie still matter? I'd argue that it's earned its place – through graft, loyalty, energy and character. There are few breeds quite like it.

Today, devoted owners and breeders continue to keep the breed healthy, visible and full of bounce, just as Mrs Willison once did. In doing so, they ensure the bearded collie holds its own where it belongs – among Scotland's distinctive, treasured breeds.

WHEN HEATHER MET PEGGY

Some dogs saunter into your life but not Peggy. She cannonballed in, sent slippers flying, barked at a seagull (and sent that flying, too) – then spun round to see who was responsible. A three-year-old bearded collie from the famed Sallen line, Peggy – Sallen Carol, if we're standing on ceremony – lives in Edinburgh with Heather, who is under no illusion about who's in charge. "I am owned by Peggy," she says, only half joking.

Bearded collies aren't for the faint of heart – they're hill-chargers, puddle-stompers, sock-thieves who'll buffet you with enough personality to power a cèilidh band all the way through the night and into the early hours. But Heather knew exactly what she was getting into. Her dad had Beardies and her childhood was shaped by Flossie – a scruffy, big-hearted Beardie dervish. Later came Poppy, who lived to nearly nineteen and accompanied Heather everywhere, from Munro-bagging to Therapet visits in hospitals, hospices and university halls. When Poppy passed away in 2021, Heather waited, broken-hearted – it takes time to let another Beardie-shaped bundle back into your life.

Then came Peggy. She was bred by Nic and Nell Broadbridge in Lanark – stalwarts of the breed since the 1960s – and from the start she showed signs of being a classic Beardie (plus ever so slightly bonkers). At home, Peggy plays it cool – she's fond of socks (especially ones fresh from cycling shoes) and specialises in the crafty art of sneak theft by which she gathers all manner of stuff to her bed. But outside, she lets loose, with a tail powered by pure jubilation and a Richter-scale blast of energy.

She greets her friends – human or hound – with a bum wiggle and a hop, like coiled springs are hiding in her heels. Heather says the full Beardie bounce is still a work in progress, but with her endless pizazz, she'll definitely get there! Peggy has her rituals, too. At six sharp every morning, Heather receives a nose boop to the face – no snooze button, no negotiation: it's breakfast time. Peggy's menu is not standard dog fayre; she likes watermelon, cucumber, blueberries and yoghurt.

Then Peggy keeps Heather company while she works from home, before demanding proper adventures come clocking-off time. They roam the Cairngorms together, scrambling forest trails and making the most of Scotland's generous wilderness. Coastal walks are a favourite, especially those where there's space to run, shout into the wind and chase a gull or two for good measure.

Their first Munro together is immortalised in a windswept summit photo:

two silhouettes against the clouds on Schiehallion, both grinning like loons. It sits on Heather's bookcase now – a symbol of many more peaks to be bagged.

So what makes Peggy special? Heather says it's her joy, her sheer unapologetic enthusiasm for everyday things. The bark at a drifting leaf and the gusto with which she greets a new trail. "She's my sidekick," Heather says. "Crazy, beautiful and completely herself." And that's the heart of it. Peggy is a bearded collie through and through – independent but loyal, chaotic and clever, and with a heart big enough to carry you through the darkest days. Theirs is a true partnership, and Heather wouldn't have it any other way.

AUNTIE KAREN

Not every dog belongs to just one person. Some, like Oskar, gather a whole circle of humans around them – each one just a little bit in love. Eighteen months old and already a real character, Oskar is a bearded collie of enthusiasm, energy and heart. He's not Karen's dog, but you'd never know it. "I'm Auntie Karen," she says proudly. "I help with walks, give cuddles and basically borrow him as often as I can."

Karen and her husband Mark are lifelong dog lovers. When their twin boys were little, they brought home two Jack Russells – Taz and Tiny – who stayed with them until they passed away at the incredible age of nineteen. "They were family," Karen says. "After they died, I couldn't imagine getting another dog until I retire. So having Oskar to help with is perfect."

From the moment they met, Oskar made an impression. "He was popped on my lap – and promptly peed all over me," Karen says. "So I felt the warmth of his love right from the start!" Since then, he's become a fixture in her life. Oskar is the very picture of Beardie exuberance – affectionate, excitable, uninterested in doing what he's told and endlessly friendly to every dog he meets. He's a master of mess, preferring puddle water to a clean bowl and always choosing the boggiest patch of ground to roll in.

"If there's mud, he'll find it," Karen says. "And if there's an audience, he'll ignore it. He won't pose. He won't perform. Not unless there's food involved – and even then, it's on his terms."

And yet, despite his wild ways, Oskar has a tender streak – he seeks out company, leans into touch and knows exactly how to wrap people round his paw. "He's just such a softie," Karen says. "Loveably nuts, but soft." Helping care for Oskar has brought a joyful companionship back into Karen's life – a dose of daily silliness, long walks and a whole lot of love. "I don't have a dog right now," she says. "But I do have Oskar. And that's more than enough."

So here's to the dog aunties, uncles, neighbours and borrowed humans – the extended family who walk, feed, cuddle and care. It really does take a village, and dogs all over Scotland are all the happier for the extra love you bring into their lives.

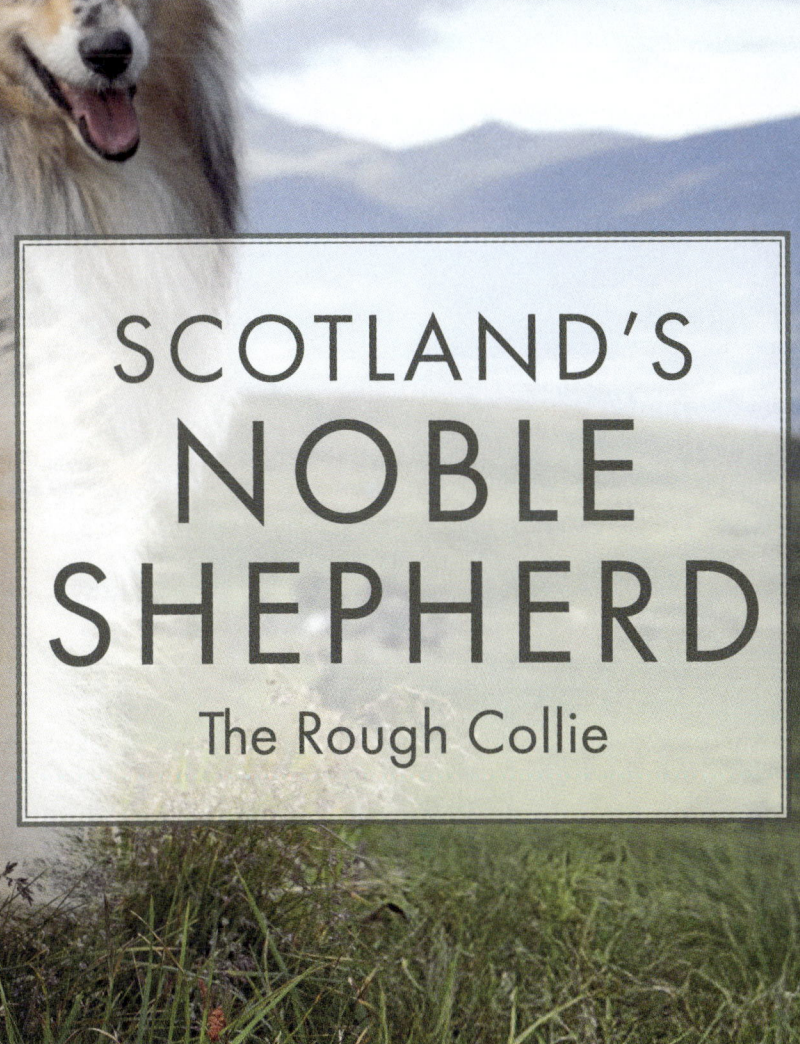

SCOTLAND'S NOBLE SHEPHERD

The Rough Collie

BREED STANDARD

GENERAL APPEARANCE: Elegant, balanced, with a proud carriage and intelligent expression.
COAT: Abundant double coat with soft, dense undercoat and straight, harsh outer coat.
COLOUR: Sable and white, tricolour, blue merle, white with coloured markings.
EYES: Medium-sized, almond-shaped, dark except in blue merles.
MOVEMENT: Effortless, graceful and ground-covering with good drive.
TEMPERAMENT: Friendly, affectionate, loyal and responsive

A NAME ROOTED IN SCOTTISH SOIL

At first glance, the rough collie might seem like a dog bred for show – all flowing coat and soft-eyed charm, but don't be fooled. Behind the elegance lies a true working breed, rooted in the terrain of Scotland. Trusted by generations of farming folk, this dog was valued not for looks, but for its ability to manage livestock across open ground with intelligence, instinct and dependability. Like so many of Scotland's breeds, the rough collie began as a stalwart farm helper.

The very name *collie* has ancient roots. Some say it comes from the old Scots word colley or coaly, meaning coal-black; others suggest a Gaelic origin, from cùilean, meaning puppy. Whatever its source, by the time the rough collie took shape, *collie* had come to mean one thing across Scotland – a sharp-eyed sheepdog and a farmer's right hand on four legs.

For generations, these herding dogs were known simply as Scotch collies or farm collies, and they varied in looks. Many were predominantly black or two-tone with black and tan markings; some had brindle or sable coats, and most had shorter, harsher hair than the elegant rough collie we recognise today. But all shared that keen instinct to herd and a relentless devotion to duty. They were a common sight as they drove sheep and cattle to market or bounded along beside horse-drawn carts on country roads. However, in the mid-1800s, this pastoral Scottish breed began to catch the public's eye – and nothing would ever be the same again.

THE RISE OF THE SHOW COLLIE

With the increase in the popularity of dog shows, collies were soon appearing in the ring. Breeders began refining their appearance, favouring a more elegant silhouette – longer muzzle, narrower face and a fuller, more dramatic coat. It was rumoured that some early breeders crossed their collies with Russian borzoi sighthounds to create a more aristocratic head shape. We'll never know if this is fact or folklore, as there is no definitive genetic or documentary proof, and many breed historians argue the transformation was achieved through selective breeding alone, rather than crossbreeding. Whatever the method, the result was clear. The rough collie's look became more elongated and refined, with the long tapering snout and distinctive mane of fur that remains their hallmark today.

THE IMPACT OF OLD COCKIE

By 1873, the Kennel Club was formally registering rough collies, and one of the dogs most responsible for setting the

GROUP: Pastoral.
STATUS: Stable, but considerably lower than in previous decades.
ORIGIN: Bred in Scotland for farm work, the rough collie was shaped as a smart, resilient herding dog with a distinctive, flowing coat.
HEIGHT: Male: 56–61 cm. Female: 51–56 cm
WEIGHT: Male: 27–34 kg. Female: 23–30 kg.

Socialisation
Friendliness
Trainability

Size

Colour

> **DID YOU KNOW? ROUGH COLLIE CURIOSITIES**
> - **Lassie's Leading Man:** Onscreen, Lassie was always portrayed as female, but in reality the role was played by a male rough collie named Pal (and later Pal's male descendants). These male dogs were chosen partly for their fuller coats and slightly larger size.
> - **Marilyn Meet Lassie:** Even Marilyn Monroe found herself charmed. In 1952, she was photographed meeting Pal at a Hollywood party – a brief encounter between two icons of their time.
> - **Before Lassie, There Was Lad:** Some say the stage was set for Eric Knight's Lassie by Albert Payson Terhune, who first cast rough collies as literary heroes. His early twentieth-century stories, including Lad – A Dog, turned his own collies into fictional stars and helped define the breed's esteemed reputation in America.

breed's direction was known as Old Cockie. Thought to be the first sable, he stood out in an era when most collies were black and white, tricolour or black and tan. His rich sable and white coat, combined with a kind expression and balanced build, caused a stir at competitions. First exhibited at Birmingham, he won numerous prizes and soon became the cornerstone of many early breeding lines. Owned by James Bissell, Old Cockie lived to the age of fourteen and sired offspring that would shape the rough collie for generations to come.

But how could I even consider writing a chapter on rough collies without talking about the breed's most iconic hero? *Lassie Come-Home* by Eric Knight was first published as a short story in the Philadelphia-based magazine, *The Saturday Evening Post* – which in the 1930s enjoyed a circulation of over 3 million readers! The tale was an overnight success, and Knight expanded it into a novel, which was released in the US in 1940, and quickly afterwards in the UK.

Knight's novel told the story of a devoted collie named Lassie, belonging to a poor Yorkshire boy, who is sold to the fictitious Duke of Rudling and taken hundreds of miles away to the Scottish Highlands – only to escape and make the long journey home, overcoming every obstacle through sheer ingenuity.

> **Tigh gun chù gun chat gun leanabh beag, tigh gun ghean gun ghàire.**
>
> *A house without a dog, a cat, or a little child is a house without affection or merriment.*

> **DID YOU KNOW? ROUGH COLLIE CURIOSITIES**
> - **A Rough Collie in the White House:** Rob Roy, a striking white rough collie, belonged to First Lady Grace Coolidge and became a fixture of presidential life. He was often seen at her side during state dinners, and his calm presence was immortalised in a famous 1924 portrait that still hangs in the China Room of the White House today.
> - **Quieter Than You Think:** Rough collies are known to "talk" – sighing, chuffing, gently yipping and softly "woo-wooing" rather than constant barking.

Released just as the Second World War broke out, the story struck a powerful chord: its themes of separation, endurance and reunion resonated with readers facing upheaval and uncertainty in their own lives.

LASSIE – A STAR IS BORN

Hollywood took notice and in 1943, MGM released *Lassie Come Home*, a Technicolor film adaptation starring a striking rough collie in the title role, alongside young actors Roddy McDowall and Elizabeth Taylor. Audiences, weary from the war, were enchanted. Here was a dog who would swim rivers, traverse mountains and brave any danger to reunite with the child she loved.

Lassie transcended her character in the film. In the hearts of viewers and society at large, she became *the* dog – a fearless emblem of unwavering loyalty and intelligence. And we need a round of applause for Pal, the male doggy actor playing our canine heroine who gave performances so instinctively tuned to the needs of the scene that he simply *became* Lassie in the public imagination.

Pal went on to star in a series of Lassie films, before passing the role to his descendants. In 1954, Lassie made the leap to television in the form of a weekly show that would run for nineteen years, making it one of the most watched shows in the world, with viewers in over a hundred countries

TRAINING THE LEGEND

The dogs playing Lassie were trained by Rudd Weatherwax, a former vaudeville and early film-animal trainer, who developed a method of working with collies using hand signals and whispered commands. It's said that Pal could perform more than two hundred cues – far more than most animal actors of the time.

The cultural impact was enormous. Demand for rough collies soared, especially in North America and Europe, as families wanted a "Lassie dog" of their own – a loyal friend, gentle with children and always ready to lend a paw. Even now, Lassie is an instantly recognisable icon of pop culture.

CHARACTER & DEVOTION
It's quite remarkable that a Scottish herding dog, once a fixture of a tough farming life, shape-shifted to become a movie star and international emblem of what a family means – even earning a coveted star on the Hollywood Walk of Fame. But beyond the glam and glitz of film and TV, real-life rough collies continued to be loving pets and farm workers, with some working as early guide dogs for the visually impaired.

The breed's gentle disposition and intuitive nature make it well-suited to working closely with people. Sometimes they can seem near-human in understanding – knowing when to play the clown to cheer someone up, or when to stand protectively between a child and danger. The world came to appreciate and adore these dogs in a fictional setting, but in Scotland folks would simply nod "aye" in response to praise being

showered upon the breed; for them, it goes without saying that collies are truly special.

GENTLE GUARDIANSHIP
One of the rough collie's most cherished traits is its gentleness; a well-socialised collie is patient and tolerant, and after an initial alert, they mostly prefer to win over strangers with a quick sniff and a good-natured wag. Their deep bark can sound formidable when someone knocks at the door – "who's there?" they seem to say – yet moments later they are bouncing around their guest in delightful welcome.

A charming quirk you'll often see is the collie's impulse to herd moving things – be it chasing at the heels of kids playing, rounding up ducks by the pond or even the family cat (much to the cat's dismay). Such behaviours are a reminder that in every collie is an ever-vigilant worker, raring to go.

CARING FOR THE MAGNIFICENT COAT

Living with a rough collie can mean embracing a bit of fur and outdoor debris as part of the deal, but it's more than worth it. That fine coat, flowing like a mane with its feathery bloomers on the legs, does require upkeep. Set aside time to brush from head to tail – and you'll find the dog often relishes the attention, as if it were an indulgent spa treatment. Collies shed seasonally: usually a heavy blow of coat in spring and a smaller one in autumn. The dogs seem to take pride in keeping themselves clean, fastidiously licking any spots of dirt away.

Exercise needs are moderate. Rough collies are not as relentlessly high-energy as their Border collie kin, but nor are they lazy. Daily walks and some playtime are essential. A well-exercised collie makes for a polite, contented housemate, happy to lounge. They are quite adaptable to different living situations, whether city, coastal or countryside. They don't *need* acres of land to roam, but they do need regular outings.

Perhaps the most important aspect of caring for a rough collie is the companionship itself: they thrive on being part of the family unit. They don't tend to do well if left alone for long stretches day after day – they can become lonely and are likely to grow very vocal about it. If your lifestyle keeps you away for more than a few hours, a collie will need a dog walker or neighbourly visitor to break up the solitude for them.

Happy collies are incredibly rewarding friends: they'll listen to you blether, trot along on errands, and offer endless affection. Live with a rough collie, and you'll likely find yourself chatting to your dog as you would an old pal – and in their own calm way, they'll show you they understand. Yet the breed has suffered a 94 per cent decline in UK registrations since its 1970s peak of around eight thousand puppies a year. Today, the rough collie numbers hover precariously low – a far cry from the breed's heyday. The Rough Collie Breed Council – a union of fifteen accredited clubs across the UK – works tirelessly to preserve and promote the breed.

PEOPLE WITH DOGS MAKE GLASGOW

There's something majestic about a rough collie at rest . . . they possess a gentle serenity that settles across their shoulders like a cloak. For Paul and Stephen of Crookston, Glasgow, that regal presence has graced their lives for over a decade now, ever since the unexpected arrival of two very special dogs.

Andy and Summer, both sable and white rough collies, came to them in July 2011 through a friend whose cousin had sadly passed away. It was a bittersweet beginning – two dogs urgently needing a new home – but it became a transformative moment. "They'd lived in Singapore," Paul recalls, "and Andy had originally come from Siberia, so they were pretty worldly by the time they arrived with us. We just fell in love with them."

For twelve years, Andy and Summer were a devoted duo – full of character and that particular collie charisma that seems to slow the world down a little. Their passing, in 2022 and 2023, left an enormous hole. But, as anyone who's lived through that kind of grief will understand, it also left a certainty – they would have dogs again. And love, when it's shared so completely, has a way of returning, particularly when you've already been charmed by a Scottish breed as magical as the rough collie.

Enter Gio – a six-year-old blue merle male with the Kennel Club name KingPin Kourika – who joined the family in January 2024. He came from respected rough collie breeder, Robin Blaikie in Cheltenham, already a champion and even a grandfather, but with a heart still open to a new beginning. "Like most collies, he was quite shy at first," Stephen says. "It took about three weeks and then this steady, delightful character really began to shine through. He's incredibly friendly, loves children and, honestly, he'd make the perfect therapy dog." Indeed, there's something thoughtfully intuitive about Gio. He's a dog who reads the room, and his instincts were never more needed than when Florence arrived later that year.

Two-year-old Florence – aka Avonfair A Million Dreams – is a sable and white rough collie from Michelle Mitchell, a breeder in Hamilton. She joined the household in September 2024, full of potential but bursting with nerves. On her second day, she bolted! Cue two humans, two fields of mud, one bush and one very indignant collie. "Her face said it all – outrage!" Paul laughs. "But three weeks later, we started to see the real Florence."

And what a dog she is – mischievous, playful, affectionate – and never one to miss an opportunity when food's about. "We do have to watch her near the kitchen," Stephen adds. "She once pulled down a whole cooked chicken. Straight onto herself. She was delighted."

Together, Gio and Florence have formed the sort of bond that can't be rushed. It's layered with mutual respect, a little mischief and that companionable love that's so unique to dogs. This is a household guided by an abiding affection and respect for dogs, and where what binds them all is a steady sense of pack gratitude – for the years shared and the daily joy of living with dogs like Gio and Florence, who make the world feel that bit kinder. "We just hope we have a long and happy life with them," Paul says.

GRACE AND GRIT

The Smooth Collie

BREED STANDARD

GENERAL APPEARANCE: Elegant, active dog with no trace of coarseness. Smooth outline and symmetrical.
COAT: Short, dense, flat and harsh to the touch. Weather-resistant.
COLOUR: Sable and white, tricolour and blue merle.
EYES: Medium-sized, almond-shaped, dark except in blue merles where one or both may be blue.
MOVEMENT: Effortless, with good reach and drive. Covers ground with grace and power.
TEMPERAMENT: Friendly, responsive, intelligent and loyal.

THE UNSUNG SIBLING

If the rough collie is the one in the velvet cloak, the smooth collie is the one in the waxed jacket – same poise, similar mindset, but leaner, cleaner and with a lot less fuss. Often overlooked, the smooth carries its own cool charisma. For those who know the breed, it's the best-kept secret in the dog world – graceful, loyal, intelligent and refreshingly low-maintenance. It can do everything the others can, but without the circus or any of the fanfare. And did I mention their dignified beauty?

With only twenty-nine puppies registered in 2024, the smooth collie is classed as a vulnerable native breed by the Kennel Club – the rarest of Scotland's recognised dogs. To their admirers, they are more than a hidden gem, they are the unicorn of Scottish breeds: elegant, elusive and unforgettable.

The smooth collie never needed noise to prove its worth; it moves through the world with purpose. As social media algorithms guide dog ownership trends, this breed only asks to be seen for its essence, not its spectacle. If you're thinking of welcoming a puppy into your life, consider the smooth collie. Rare doesn't mean impossible, and this treasure of a breed deserves a place in the story of Scotland's future, not just its past.

THE ROUGH WITH THE SMOOTH

Smooth and rough collies share the same roots – they are hill dogs from the Scottish farming tradition, developed to herd sheep and cattle. As the Victorian era refined the rough collie's coat for show purposes, some breeders maintained a shorter-coated version better suited to work, weather and utility. These eventually became known as the smooth collie – a distinct breed in the UK Kennel Club's eyes, but still closely linked to its longer-haired kin.

In the 1860s and 1870s, Queen Victoria became fond of smooth-haired collie-type dogs, especially during her stays at Balmoral, and it's believed she owned a grand total of eighty-eight collies over her lifetime. She kept many breeds, but on that evidence it would be fair to say that the queen loved her collies! On 3 April 1886, she noted in her journal: "I was photographed alone with my faithful Sharp." The photograph became a popular carte-de-visite, widely sold to the public like a postcard. A lifelong dog lover, Queen Victoria became Patron of the RSPCA shortly after ascending the throne in 1837, and in 1885 she also accepted patronage of Battersea Dogs' Home.

Many shepherds preferred the smooth collie – fewer thorns and sticks

GROUP: Pastoral.
STATUS: Extremely vulnerable.
ORIGIN: Developed alongside the Rough collie in Scotland, the Smooth collie was bred for herding and farm work, prized for its intelligence and short, easy-care coat.
HEIGHT: Male: 56–61 cm. Female: 51–56 cm.
WEIGHT: Male: 20.5–29.5 kg. Female: 18–25 kg.

Socialisation
Friendliness
Trainability

Size

Colour

lodged in its coat, less drying time and every bit as much brain power. Indeed, they are savvy and collected – independent quick thinkers who can problem solve and negotiate any situation. But as the rough became a family favourite and film star, the smooth slipped into the background; there remain those who love this breed, but sadly today it's one of Scotland's most underappreciated canine assets.

A DISTINCT PATH FROM SHARED ROOTS

The smooth collie shares its ancestry with the rough collie and, before that, with the broader family of Scottish pastoral dogs. Both descend from the same working stock, later diverging through selective breeding and coat preference. One of the earliest collies exhibited at the 1861 Birmingham Dog Show may have been a smooth-coated type, although we can't know for sure as early records did not distinguish coat lengths.

For many decades, rough and smooth collies were shown together, with coat length the only visible difference. The Collie Club, founded in 1881, represented both types. Separate classes began appearing in the early twentieth century, and in 1955, the Smooth Collie Club of Great Britain was formed to champion the smooth-coated variety.

DID YOU KNOW? SMOOTH COLLIE CURIOSITIES

- **A Smooth Operator:** Smooth collies favour grace over intensity, poise over pushiness. Their working style is measured, responsive and steady.
- **The Shepherd's Secret:** Highland shepherds often preferred smooths for their low-maintenance coats and field practicality.
- **Gentle Communicators:** Smooth collies are soft communicators. They use sighs, nudges and quiet grumbles and read the room rather than rule it.
- **Kelpie Cousins:** Smooth-coated collies were among the dogs exported to Australia in the nineteenth century, and they are believed to have helped shape the kelpie and Australian cattle dog.

By comparison, the Shetland sheepdog was recognised in 1914, the bearded collie in 1959, and the Border collie – long evaluated by the International Sheep Dog Society for working merit – only received full Kennel Club recognition for conformation showing in 1976. All of which means that the smooth collie was one of the first collie types to enter the show ring, but it was also one whose distinct identity required time and persistent advocacy to secure. It wasn't until 1979 that the Kennel Club allocated the first challenge certificates for smooth collies as a separate breed, and, despite its rarity, in recent years the breed has enjoyed increased popularity in the show ring, with its sound movements and placid temperament gaining many admirers.

A PAIR OF GENES

Though smooth and rough collies share roots, they are treated differently across the world. As we've seen, in the UK, the Kennel Club recognises them as two separate breeds, a classification formally adopted in 1994. Under these rules, they have distinct breed standards and cannot be interbred.

So what exactly distinguishes them? Here's the science: genetically, it comes down to a single coat gene. The long coat (*l*) is recessive: rough collies are *ll*, while smooth collies are either *Ll* or *LL*.

> **SMOOTH COLLIE SPOTLIGHT**
>
> **Breaking Ground:** Foxearth High Frequency – affectionately known as Ben – was a tricolour smooth collie born in 2002 who earned multiple UK challenge certificates and achieved the prestigious UK Champion title. At a time when the tricolour variety was seldom seen in top-level competition, his success helped raise awareness and renew interest in the breed.
>
> **Keeping the Flame Alive:** The Smooth Collie Club of Great Britain promotes the breed and encourages sound, temperament-focused breeding. It runs a dedicated judges education programme aligned with Kennel Club standards, ensuring knowledgeable assessment of the breed.
>
> **Lifeline for Collies:** Collie Rescue (Rough and Smooth) is a UK-based charity that rescues, provides veterinary care, and rehomes rough and smooth collies. The charity places around 150 to 200 dogs into loving homes each year.

Functionally, both types share the same conformation, dimensions and general temperament, but in the UK, the regulatory separation has created distinct breeding populations, each with its own identity and following.

ACROSS BORDERS

The Collie Club of America, founded in 1886 (just two years after the American Kennel Club) is one of the oldest breed-specific clubs in the States and represents both rough and smooth collies as two coat varieties under a single standard. This shared framework allows for collaboration between the two varieties, with inter-variety breeding permitted – and some say this helps to refine conformation, support genetic health and maintain consistent temperament.

While smooths remain less common than their flowing-coated cousins, they have been gaining some ground in shows and homes on both sides of the pond – thanks to the dedication of breeders all around the world who value structure, soundness and the breed's dependable nature.

Today, some of the strongest smooth collie lines can be found in Scandinavia, where breeders have championed these dogs with determination. In Sweden and Finland especially, smooths are valued not only for their elegance and utility, but also for their steady character. Health testing, thoughtful selection and clarity of purpose have helped these kennels produce dogs of outstanding quality – many of which have influenced breeding programmes around the world. Whether in the Scottish Highlands, the Midwest of America or the forests of the Nordic north, the smooth collie is a breed shaped by people committed to securing for this brilliant dog the future it deserves.

LIVING WITH A SMOOTH COLLIE

Owners sometimes speak of their smooth having an "on/off switch" – they are ready to leap into action or snooze by your feet, adapting to whatever the task calls for. They are adaptable, but like their other collie cousins, smooths do thrive on company. If left alone too often, they may become vocal or anxious; they are a dog bred to be an integral part of the household throng.

Life with a smooth collie is a study in peaceful intelligence. They're observant, responsive and tuned in. They love to work: not obsessively, but with calm commitment, and they shine in obedience, agility and therapy roles. Perfect for families, first-time owners or active older folk, they can adapt to rural or urban life, provided they have companionship, stimulation and a dose of daily adventure.

COAT & CARE

After a muddy walk, many smooth collies will clean themselves meticulously – and if wet, they may cheekily dry off against the furniture if you're not quick with a towel. The smooth collie's coat is low fuss – a quick weekly brush is usually enough to keep them clean and sleek, with dirt brushing out easily once they are dry. They do, however, shed seasonally so be ready with the vacuum cleaner. If you love the elegance of a collie but not the grooming demands, the smooth may be your perfect match.

HEALTH & LONGEVITY

The smooth collie is, by and large, a hardy, long-lived breed, with most dogs enjoying a lifespan of twelve to fourteen years, and sometimes beyond. As with all breeds, there are certain inherited conditions to be aware of, and responsible breeders work hard to minimise their occurrence through health testing and careful pairings.

One of the more common concerns is collie eye anomaly (CEA), a developmental issue that affects the eyes and can range from mild to more serious forms. Dermatomyositis, an inflammatory skin and muscle condition, can also occur, though less frequently, and epilepsy has been recorded occasionally within the breed. Another is the MDR1 gene mutation, which makes some smooth collies highly sensitive to certain medications. Of course, it's vital that every owner is aware of this before treatment, so it's best to speak with the clubs or your vet for advice.

Despite these concerns, the smooth collie remains a robust and resilient companion when bred with care. Like all good breeders, the smooth collie breeder will offer transparency about health testing, giving each pup the best chance at a long, healthy life.

SCOTLAND'S SMOOTH LEGACY

The smooth collie isn't loud in the ring, and maybe its principal aim in life isn't to trend online, but in the collie-friendly nooks of Scotland and the wider world, it's doing what it's always done – showing up with distinction. Might it be that one of these easy-on-the-eye and very smooth operators are waiting to walk into your life?

THEN THE RAIN CAME

Some dogs arrive as if swept into your life by the hush of fate itself. For Esme from Ayrshire, that dog is a striking smooth collie, officially known as Diamondfox Sir Galahad, though around the house he answers simply to Rain. He's two and a half now, with a gentleness and wisdom in him, almost like he's been here before.

Esme's first dog, growing up, was a tricoloured smooth collie called Finn; he was "the dog who started it all," she says fondly. She remembers the thrill of going along to obedience classes with him as a child, both of them eager to learn, enthralled as the connection between them developed. Life took her into the company of other breeds – whippets, an Italian greyhound – but the smooth collie never quite let go. The breed lingered like a tune you can't stop humming – a sleek, familiar melody lodged in her mind, waiting for airplay again.

That airplay came years later, sparked by a phrase Esme read in the breed standard: "*Friendly disposition with no trace of nervousness or aggressiveness.*" That was it – the essence of what she'd been looking for: a dog who was not only beautiful, but kind. Ready to meet the world with soft eyes and a steady heart.

Rain turned out to be all that and more. "He's incredibly balanced," Esme says. "He's solid, eager to please. He's calm and composed in the show ring – but out in the field, he lights up. Full of confidence, full of life." That duality – poise and play – encapsulates what drew her back to the breed. At home, he's a charming clown. "He's always presenting a toy, always up for a game or a bit of training. The tail never stops."

Rain shares his days with Ivy, a delicate Italian greyhound, and their friendship is one of pure affection. "They're such opposites, but they adore each other. It's lovely to watch – whether they're curled up together or flying across the grass at full tilt."

Rain was born in Finland, a country with a deep commitment to thoughtful dog breeding under the stewardship of the Fédération Cynologique Internationale (FCI). In FCI nations, dogs are not just judged on conformation; instead, traditional style herding trials are also available as an optional way to showcase a dog's natural working ability. For the smooth collie that can mean demonstrating both herding instinct and elegance. "Training sheep herding with Rain has been, and continues to be, an absolute joy," Esme says. "It's like we're discovering something together – not just instinct, but connection."

Of all the memories she's gathered, one stands out and that is the day Rain came home. "After so long of wishing and planning, that moment meant everything," she says. "It still does. He walked into the house as if he'd always been meant to find us."

He has his quirks, of course – those idiosyncrasies that give a dog its almost-human personality. He yawns with theatrical flair, letting out a wee dramatic noise just to draw a chuckle. If the bed isn't quite right, or the beach digging spot's a bit off, he "grumbles" to himself in low protest. "He's so expressive," Esme laughs. "He doesn't demand attention, but he knows exactly how to get it."

Whether he's weaving through heather, leaping dunes or turning heads in the show ring, this dog is radiant. Rain is a dog you can learn from, and, for Esme, he is more than a companion, he's a return to a breed – one of those pleasing, smooth circles that give life shape and meaning. He's the type of Rain that Scotland would be lucky to see more of.

SHADOW ON THE SHORE

The Shetland Sheepdog

BREED STANDARD

GENERAL APPEARANCE: Refined, symmetrical and alert, with an expression of sweetness and intelligence.
COAT: Double-coated with a long, straight, harsh outer coat with a soft and dense undercoat.
COLOUR: Sable and white, tricolour, blue merle, black and white, or black and tan.
EYES: Medium, almond-shaped, dark (except in merles), set obliquely with intelligent expression.
MOVEMENT: Effortless, smooth, ground-covering with drive from hindquarters.
TEMPERAMENT: Intelligent, affectionate, responsive, reserved with strangers but never nervous.

THE LITTLEST CROFTER

Stark in the Northern Atlantic light, standing firm on the edge of a voe, ears pricked, coat lifted by the wind, eyes fixed on the flock . . . the Sheltie earned its spot on Shetland's rugged shoreline, not as an ornament, but as a grafter.

Bred for life in a land of peaty moor, craggy shoreline and – let's be honest – challenging, often unforgiving weather, the Shetland sheepdog is sure-footed, clever and loyal. Like the famed (and adorable) ponies and cattle of the Northern Isles, the dogs that herded them also evolved to be diminutive in stature. Despite their rather fairytale appearance – with flowing coats and a foxy elegance – Shelties are not delicate or dainty. They are always-alert herders, built for nimble movement over uneven ground and for working in harsh, exposed conditions. Beneath that bonnie coat, they are not afraid of toil. Once the Sheltie was an essential part of everyday Shetland life: herding sheep, guarding homesteads and keeping each croft day ticking along. Though they now grace living rooms and city streets around the world, their story begins in those Northern Isles – where beauty and utility go hand in hand, and where they were shaped.

WEATHERPROOF BEAUTY

The Sheltie's weatherproof coat – a

double-layered marvel that evokes salt spray on the wind – is perhaps its stand-out feature. Having evolved to withstand Shetland's fiercest gales, the outer coat is long, straight and harsh to the touch – designed to repel rain or snow – while the undercoat is soft and dense, providing essential insulation.

Colours vary and are part of the breed's visual appeal. Shelties can be, for example, sable and white, blue merle, tricolour and black and white. Each coat has its own magic, but none are for vanity. The Sheltie's striking appearance is a practicality as much as a glory.

Regular grooming is desirable, especially around the neck ruff, hocks and hind legs where mats can form. Weekly brushing and seasonal blowouts will help keep the coat in good condition. Remember, too, that the Sheltie is a clean dog by nature, very diligent in self-preening, though their long fur is a magnet for debris in the wild and they may need help removing stoor.

HEALTH & HEART

As well as handsome, Shetland sheepdogs are generally healthy and hardy. They are long-lived, often reaching twelve to fifteen years, with many going well beyond. However, like many purebred dogs, they are unfortunately prone to certain genetic conditions.

GROUP: Pastoral.
STATUS: Stable but low, with signs of a gradual decline.
ORIGIN: From the Shetland Islands, the Shetland sheepdog was bred as a small, agile herder capable of managing flocks in harsh, windswept terrain.
HEIGHT: Male: 37 cm. Female: 35.5 cm.
WEIGHT: 6–12 kg.

> **DID YOU KNOW?**
> **SHELTIE CURIOSITIES**
> - **The Toonie Dug:** Before it was called the Shetland sheepdog, this breed was known locally as the "Toonie Dug". Toon in Shetland dialect meaning a small farmstead or field (which is distinct from Scots toon for town!).
> - **Small Beginnings:** Early Shelties were peerie wee at just 20 to 25 cm tall, making them ideal for crofting life where smaller dogs needed less to eat but could still do the work.
> - **Singing with the Wind:** Their famously high-pitched bark once served to cut through Shetland winds, helping move sheep or alert crofters.
> - **Cloaked in Colour:** Sheltie coats range from sable to tricolour, bi-black and the distinctive blue merle. Each pattern is rooted in coat genetics and, as some say more poetically, these are shades that echo island skies.

As a herding breed, Shelties benefit from daily exercise and mental enrichment. Walks, fetch games, trick training and scent work all help keep them content. They are not typically high-energy in the manner of some larger collie types, but do need consistent outlets for their bright minds and agile bodies.

VIKING ROOTS & NORDIC KIN

Look into the past of these dogs, and it's easy to picture their ancestors arriving by longship. When Norse settlers came to Shetland in the eighth and ninth centuries, they brought more than axes and sagas. They also brought sheep, ponies and hardy working dogs, companions as vital to survival as any blade or bannock. These early dogs were likely small, intelligent and resilient, sharing ancestry with the fluffy Spitz-type herders of Scandinavia – the Icelandic sheepdog, the Norwegian buhund and the Swedish vallhund – all dogs of a type, with pointed ears, thick coats and a sturdy, compact frame suited to northern lands.

While direct lineage is impossible to prove, many breed historians agree that these Scandinavian herding dogs formed part of the genetic bedrock from which the Shetland sheepdog sprang. Their descendants were shaped further

through generations of crossbreeding with working Scottish collies. Some sources suggest that toy breeds – such as Pomeranians – were introduced in later years to reduce size and enhance coat texture, eventually creating the compact, quick-witted Sheltie we know today.

Like their Nordic keepers, these dogs emerged from a world where nature did not indulge extravagance; on crofts where winter was difficult, dogs needed to think independently, move nimbly and hold their own against the cold and dark. Whether herding the native sheep or standing guard at the low longhouse doorways, we can well imagine how these dogs were shaped by the same elemental forces and northern light as their Shetland Viking masters.

THE ISLAND FORGE

By the late nineteenth century, the Sheltie began to catch the attention of mainland visitors, especially sailors and tourists who were enchanted by the island's "miniature collies". The breed's resemblance to the rough collie led many to believe they were simply scaled-down versions, but the Sheltie's development was far more nuanced.

> **DID YOU KNOW?**
> **SHELTIE CURIOSITIES**
> - **Mind Over Muscle:** Consistently ranking among the most intelligent dog breeds, Shelties excel in obedience, agility and problem-solving.
> - **A Herder's Heart:** These dogs were more than sheepdogs; they guarded gardens from stock where there were no fences and would even keep children entertained with good grace.
> - **The Great Name Debate:** The breed debuted as the "Shetland Collie" in 1909, but was swiftly renamed after discussions with rough collie breeders seeking to avoid any confusion.
> - **Miley's Merle:** Pop star Miley Cyrus had a blue merle Sheltie named Emu. The dog appeared in music videos, and the singer even has a tattoo of him on her arm.

The Sheltie undoubtedly shares ancestry with the broader Collie family, in particular the rough collie who some claim was intentionally used to refine the Sheltie's appearance and temperament for Kennel Club recognition. We will never know for sure, but this refinement probably softened some of the breed's rugged, Shetlander individuality.

In 1908, in Lerwick, the Shetland Collie Club held their first meetings in an effort to preserve the breed. The following year, they requested Kennel Club recognition for the dogs, but were refused. Then the club changed their name to the Scottish Shetland Sheepdog Club and produced their own stud book, effectively providing a standard for the breed. Thanks to the work of this group, the Kennel Club finally recognised the Sheltie as a distinct pedigree in 1914.

A FIRESIDE COMPANION

Though no longer a common croft dog, the Shetland sheepdog still carries the spirit and industriousness of island life, where you may need to work that wee bit harder. Whether they are out running, chasing a ball or resting by the homely blaze of a peat fire, the Sheltie remains true to its island roots: a working dog with a hint of trow dust in its coat.

THE BEST WEE BOY EVER

Ghillie arrived like the clap of Thor's hammer and instantly ruled the roost. Just three years old, he's a gorgeous sable and lives in the Royal Burgh of Renfrew, where his role is threefold: protector, shadow and best boy.

Ghillie was born during the final days of the late Queen's life and his name – Ghillie na Bànrigh, "The Ghillie to the Queen" – resonates with royal and personal weight. It's a nod to the queen of Mark's household: Piper, the family's first Sheltie, who passed away not long after Ghillie arrived. "He was in awe of her," says Mark. "She ruled the house and he followed her every move."

When she was just a tiny pup, Piper chose Mark. He was fifteen and she climbed into his lap and refused to leave. When Piper had a single daughter, Grace, the two became a devoted mother-and-daughter duo, joining the family on their Munro-bagging expeditions and lighting up the lives of his late gran and great-aunt in their care homes.

Ghillie came next; first as Piper's companion in her twilight years, then as the home's new heartbeat. "He's loud," Mark says with a laugh. "But he's also one of the most loving, protective little souls you could ever meet." During the day, Ghillie is full of beans – chasing balls, striding out on long walks and keeping a close eye on any and all passers-by. But come evening, he softens entirely and he'll curl up beside you.

"No one is allowed to hug my mum," Mark says. "Not without him appearing out of nowhere to tell us off. He huffs, grumbles and lets out this little scolding bark – like we've overstepped."

Ghillie's sense of loyalty runs deep – and when it's tested, he doesn't forget. In 2024, Mark moved temporarily to the United States for work while Ghillie stayed home. Ghillie refused to engage with Mark's regular video calls. "He would just walk off in a full strop."

When Mark returned for good, the reunion was fierce. "He cried," says Mark. "And didn't leave my side for a week." But now, Ghillie's not taking any chances. "If I so much as pick up my keys, he barks. If I put my shoes on, he huffs. He's not letting me disappear again."

For all his drama and devotion, Ghillie's abiding, soulful presence really does make him special. "I was probably the most nervous before we got him," Mark admits. "After two girls, the idea of a boy Sheltie felt like unknown territory. But he's been an absolute godsend. He's this man's best friend. The best wee boy ever."

Ghillie has got his family wrapped right around his furry wee paw, which is precisely as it should be.

THE SHEPHERD'S COMPANION

The Border Collie

BREED STANDARD

GENERAL APPEARANCE: Lean, athletic, and built for stamina and precision, with a harmonious balance of strength and grace.
COAT: Double-coated – may be rough or smooth, but is always weather-resistant.
COLOUR: Commonly black and white, but also red, blue merle, tricolour and more.
EYES: Wide-set, oval, intelligent and observant.
MOVEMENT: Effortless, smooth and controlled with a gliding, ground-covering stride.
TEMPERAMENT: Highly intelligent, responsive, alert, keen to work and quick to learn.

MIND LIKE WIND

Before a Border collie moves, the still air seems to hang thick with instinct. They are so attuned to their task that you can feel the buzz of intent in their stealth and pre-emptive glances. Then, through the hush, with a focus and flow as natural as rain falling on Ben Nevis – it begins. Not to run, or to bound, but to move in a way more akin to gliding – with ears pricked, body low and eyes transfixed by the flock.

Of all the dogs in this wee book, the Border collie is perhaps the last one that still actively and commonly practises the task it was bred for. At any farm or smallholding the length and breadth of Scotland, you are likely to see a Border collie at work. These dogs are the result of centuries of breeding, which has been fine-tuned to perfection by the understanding between shepherd and canine companion. To see one diligently, masterfully moving sheep feels like a rare, authentic honour. No other breed has carried the working soul of Scotland so gracefully into the modern age.

THE DOG THAT READS THE WIND

Border collies operate in a way that comes close to the mystical; there is no barking, no chaos, no snapping at heels. Instead, there is piercing eye contact – an unblinking stare that holds sheep in thrall – and the ability to move the herd with the slightest shift of weight, a motion almost too nuanced to see. The Border commands through subtlety not force.

The term "strong eye", which describes their ability to fix gaze on livestock and control them through presence alone, is central to the breed's language. Yet, for all their precision, Border collies are not robotic; rather, they adapt, they decide, they think on their feet. What makes them so extraordinary is this meeting of intuition, intelligence and agility.

LIVING WITH A BORDER COLLIE

Border collies make excellent companions, but they are not for everyone, as their minds demand genuine stimulation. That clever energy requires outlet and, without meaningful work, they can become anxious, vocal or obsessive. Believe me, the last thing anyone wants is for them to be herding shadows, chasing bikes or rearranging the furniture!

But in the right home – where they're given time and attention, purpose and plenty of playful partnership – they shine. Regular ball games or long walks, to exercise both body and mind, help keep them content. They thrive in agility classes, too – so if you are already very active, you could read this as a clue that you might

GROUP: Pastoral.
STATUS: Secure.
ORIGIN: Bred along the Anglo-Scottish border, these smart collies were developed as exceptionally intelligent and tireless herding dogs, able to manage sheep across open terrain.
HEIGHT: Male: 48–56 cm. Female: 43–53 cm.
WEIGHT: Male: 14–20 kg. Female: 12–19 kg.

Socialisation
Friendliness
Trainability

Size

Colour

be a Border collie person! They're deeply loyal and affectionate, often bonding tightly to one person and always wanting to work *with* you, not for you.

FROM HILL TO HERITAGE

Our tale begins in the Scottish Borders, where rolling pasture meets hardy flocks. Early herding dogs likely arrived in the British Isles with the Romans, and over time their descendants adapted to the rougher, harsher climate of northern England and southern Scotland. By the time of the ninth-century Norse incursions, the early collie type – agile, intelligent and strong – was already central to the agricultural life of the region. We don't know the exact pairings or rationale that shaped this animal, but the goal was clear – a dog built to herd sheep. By the eighteenth and nineteenth centuries, selective breeding for hill work created the prototype of these collies who soon proved themselves indispensable. They herd like a dream, true, but perhaps most impressive of all is their next-level ability to work – flawlessly, every time – to the whistle!

THE LEGACY OF OLD HEMP

Border collie genealogy centres around the story of one dog – Old Hemp. Born in 1893 in Northumberland to a dog named Roy and a female named Meg, and bred by Adam Telfer, Old Hemp was a worker of intense and extraordinary instinct. He was neither loud nor forceful; instead, he moved with calm precision, using eye and presence rather than bark or bite. By the time he was a year old, he was trialling, and his skills quickly became the benchmark for all Border collies.

Old Hemp didn't just work differently. He redefined what a good sheepdog could be. His method, combining utter focus with uncanny stock sense, became the model for future generations. Telfer, recognising something exceptional, bred him extensively but carefully. Old Hemp carried something vital for the breed – a balance of instinct, discipline and temperament – and went on to sire over two hundred puppies.

Today, nearly every pedigree Border collie traces back to him. More than a founder, Old Hemp was a blueprint. At every trial held across the hills and pastures of the working world, his legacy walks at a shepherd's side.

THE TRIALLING TRADITION

It all began in 1873, in Bala, North Wales, with the first recorded competitive sheepdog trial. On an autumn day, a curious crowd gathered to watch shepherds put their dogs to the test – not on remote hillsides, but in a flat field, marked out with gates, pens and judged obstacles.

What began as a local contest soon grew into something more. Its popularity surprised even the organisers, and in the decades that followed, the tradition of

---

DID YOU KNOW?
COLLIE CURIOSITIES

- **Leading Numbers:** The Border collie is the most registered working sheepdog in the UK, with the International Sheep Dog Society recording over 300,000 of these dogs since 1948, which is more than any other herding breed.
- **Wildlife Detectives:** Some Border collies are trained for conservation detection work in which they seek out endangered species, like bats and newts, by scent.
- **Brain Power:** In cognitive trials, Border collies have rivalled primates in problem-solving and memory. They have been known to outperform chimpanzees in certain social and practical tasks.

Is fheàirrde cù, cù a chronachadh.

A good dog will discipline another.

the work of a shepherd would be near impossible.

The society has become the global centre of excellence for working Border collies, and its focus is clear: to register, promote and protect sheepdogs bred for their ability to work stock – not for appearance or trend, but for instinct and intelligence. The society maintains a separate stud book, and its trials have long set the standard for practical, skilled herding. At competitions like the International Sheepdog Trial, handlers and dogs navigate flocks with near-telepathic teamwork. This is a living tradition and its extraordinary knowledge is often passed down through generations of farming families.

In 1976, the Kennel Club formally recognised the Border collie, paving the way for conformation showing and broader public appeal. Today, some dogs carry both registrations, while others remain within the ISDS, focused solely on working ability. Each tradition honours the breed but slightly differently – one for its versatility and temperament, the other for its function. Together, they form a framework that helps the Border collie thrive both as a beloved companion and a working legend.

the sheepdog trial spread across the UK, evolving into a public celebration of the bond between human and dog. When a dog understands its handler and moves with them as if of one mind, it stirs something deep in us – respect, pleasure and awe.

GUARDIANS OF THE WORKING COLLIE

The International Sheep Dog Society was founded in 1906 to promote the shepherd's calling and improve the management of livestock through better working dogs. And that remains its purpose today, for without a good sheepdog,

SEARCH AND RESCUE DOG ASSOCIATION SCOTLAND

Skye, an alert and spirited two-year-old Border collie, was officially graded by SARDA Scotland in March 2024. Her handler Julian, who also serves as the association's secretary, often says she has a knack for "finding lost people and greeting everyone like an old friend". This charity is entirely volunteer run and, alongside a skilled team of search dogs, Skye supports mountain rescue operations across the Highlands and Islands.

From just twelve weeks old, Skye and her colleagues – Border collies, spaniels, Labradors and other scent hounds – are trained to pair sharp noses with the soft bark that signals a rescue find. These dogs shine in the field, showing stamina, fast thinking in treacherous conditions and an exceptional skill in reading their handlers. They are a vital part of the teams bravely working to find missing or vulnerable people on Scotland's mountains and moors.

sarda-scotland.org

ONE MAN AND HIS DOG: A NATIONAL TREASURE

For decades, the working genius of the Border collie was known only to the good folk running them with sheep – but then came the cameras! In 1976, the BBC launched *One Man and His Dog*, a series that would beam sheepdog trials into millions of captivated living rooms. Narrated by naturalist and broadcaster Phil Drabble, the programme offered a subtly appealing yet compelling glimpse into the world of competitive herding. With teams from Scotland, Ireland, Wales and England, the show celebrated skills from the hills ... and it was a huge, if unexpected hit with audiences. At its height in the 1980s, viewing figures ran to over 8 million – a triumph of TV exposure for the popularity of working dogs such as collies.

Further north, a distinctly Scottish and Gàidhealach take on the tradition emerged. *Farpaisean Chon-Chaorach*, launched on BBC Alba in 2008, brought the same trials to life through the lens of crofting culture and the Gaelic language. With presenters Donald "Sweeny" MacSween and Catrìona Ruadh MacPhee, it captured not only

the skill of dog and handler, but also the rhythms of rural life and the pride of farming communities.

Together, these programmes gave the nation a front-row seat to witness the brilliance of a dog as a living tool in the art of flock management. Many remember with nostalgic fondness the hypnotic, calming yet thrilling effect of the commentary, the shepherds, their dogs and the obedient sheep being marshalled into their pens – and the high drama when the odd one decided to go off piste. It truly was landmark programming and a celebratory beacon in the

schedule for these wonderful dogs and their shepherds.

But with the rapid changes to farming life and the technology that's replacing many traditional tasks, it's hard to know what the future may hold for the working sheepdog. One thing is clear, though: Border collies – as companions, not just as colleagues on a working farm – are earning themselves more fans than ever.

DID YOU KNOW?
COLLIE CURIOSITIES

- **Wartime Hero:** Rob, a Border collie who served with the SAS during the Second World War, was awarded the PDSA Dickin Medal for bravery, making him one of the war's most decorated dogs.
- **Window Wizard:** A Border collie named Striker once set a Guinness World Record by rolling down a manual car window in just 11.34 seconds.

THE BARCALDINE BORDER COLLIE

Oban born and bred, with island roots running deep to North Uist, Chrisanne is a nurse, a dog lover and the fiercely loyal companion of Marley – a black and white Border collie with an open heart as wide as the Argyllshire sky.

Bred by Chrisanne's cousin Cathy, Marley came from working stock in Skye. "She's spoiled, devoted and incredibly cuddly," says Chrisanne. "A true house dog, but with footballer's feet and incredible intuition."

It's not always been easy. When Marley was just a year old, she grew dangerously weak and couldn't even climb the stairs. She stopped eating and ended up in intensive care between Oban and Glasgow. After weeks of worry, she was diagnosed with Imerslund-Gräsbeck syndrome, a rare B12 deficiency that causes anaemia and fatigue.

"She never cost us anything to buy," says Chrisanne, "but she's cost us a small fortune since! Worth every single penny, of course."

Chrisanne and her late husband, both nurses, administered B12 injections at home every few weeks; a necessary routine that brought them closer to Marley – and to each other. In time, Marley would return that care in ways no one could have predicted.

When Chrisanne's husband passed away suddenly, it shattered their wee family, but the dogs stood by her. Marley and her older collie, Mirren, were at her side, offering quiet, constant comfort. "They were utterly in tune with how I was feeling," Chrisanne says.

Earlier this year, Mirren passed away at the wonderful old age of fourteen. Marley was grieving too, but once again, she stayed close. "The love we have for each other is tangible," says Chrisanne. "She's my shadow."

As well as her capacity for empathy, Marley is sharp as a tack and a wee bit too clever. She's more than capable of opening doors and raiding the fridge – the latter is now firmly child-locked. She plays football like a pro, dribbling, charging, tossing the ball in the air – even entertaining herself in the garden if no one's up for a kickabout. Children dote on her, and she adores them back. She cuddles on the sofa, sneaks onto the bed at night and makes all Chrisanne's days that wee bit brighter.

Through laughter and loss, mischief and stillness, Marley has been there, a reminder that the dogs which share our lives are also there to steady us through them. Or as Chrisanne puts it, "Marley makes me laugh every single day and has helped me through some of the hardest times. For that, I will be eternally grateful."

THE ISLAND SHEPHERDESS

On the Isle of Kerrera, where the sea air sharpens the senses and the weather rolls in like a mood, lives one of the most grounded people you're ever likely to meet. Sheila runs her farm at Slaterich with the kind of strength that needs no explanation – her natural way with animals is seasoned, her intuition for livestock almost elemental.

She is the keeper of a ten-strong pack of working dogs in which there are no pets, no passengers – every one of them earns their keep on the hill and they love it. "Well, a few of them live in the house, and get molly-coddled," she admits with a laugh, "but the rest are in kennels in the byre."

We met Sheila on a rain-slicked morning, the clouds folding down into the land, blurring edges and softening sound. Out of that greyness came a quad bike, weaving up the track, and on the back were four Border collies – Eddie, Suzie, Wisp and Joey. Sheila waved as she approached; they were all soaked to the skin, but raring to go. The dogs hopped off like acrobats, each with their own style – Joey dramatic, Suzie cautious, Eddie all business and Wisp almost ghostlike. They gathered in a poised posse by the quad, then each cast Sheila a glance before making a move – like wee deputy lieutenants awaiting orders. It was clear her leadership wasn't loud, but it was absolute.

Sheila didn't bark orders because she didn't need to. With a tilt of her head and a barely whispered instruction, the pack sprang eagerly into action. They moved the sheep with grace, cohesion and an almost eerie quiet. No drama or fuss – just a poetic, purposeful dance between shepherdess, dogs and flock in which each implicitly understood their role and relationship to the other.

Slaterich is a hard-working farm on a well-weathered island, but you wouldn't hear Sheila complain. She always works with the land, not against it. Instinctively she understands her animals and their needs – and it's incredible to see how she trusts her dogs like most folk trust their hands. Trained to perfection by Sheila's empathy, warmth and wit, to watch them move those sheep felt sacred, as if we were all a part of something far older and more deeply ingrained than words.

There are women in Scotland who farm with flair, strength and a healthy dose of stubbornness. Sheila stands among them – endlessly capable and kind to her animals, the dogs working as a controlled extension of her will, nudging the sheep without contact, easing them exactly where she wants them to go.

It was a wondrous, unforgettable sight . . . the dogs sprinting, creeping, slinking and sliding until the sheep were through the gate. As Sheila drove off, I walked back to the ferry smiling, thinking to myself how lucky those dogs are to live such full, purposeful lives under her stewardship, enriched by the work they all love.

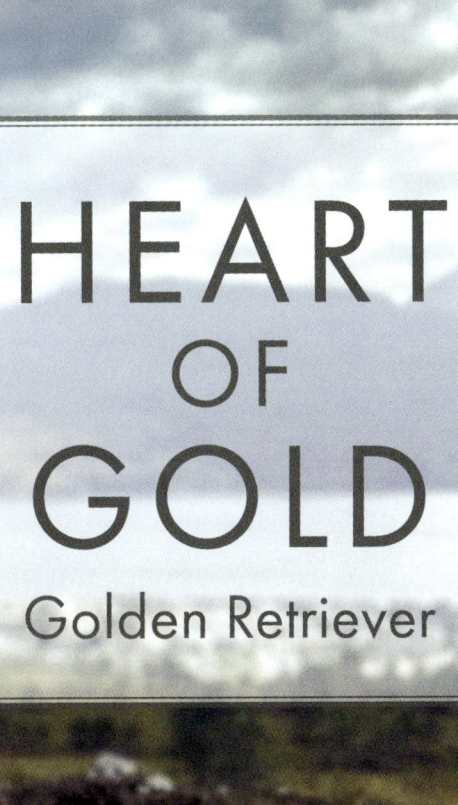

HEART OF GOLD

Golden Retriever

BREED STANDARD

GENERAL APPEARANCE: Symmetrical, balanced and powerful.
COAT: Dense water-resistant undercoat, outer coat can be wavy or flat.
COLOUR: Any shade of gold or cream, but not red or mahogany.
EYES: Dark brown with kind, intelligent expression.
MOVEMENT: Powerful, with free stride – true and straight front and rear.
TEMPERAMENT: Friendly, reliable, trustworthy, intelligent and eager to please.

A LIGHT IN THE GLEN

Golden retrievers are exceptional dogs, with their warm eyes, gentle ways and steady loyalty. No surprise, then, that they've earned a place not only in our homes, but in our hearts. It's immediately obvious upon meeting one of these beautiful animals why the word "gold" is in their name, but it reflects more than their lustrous, leonine coats. They are golden thanks to their empathy, kindness and adaptability, too.

Today, they're one of the best-loved breeds in the world, but to truly understand them, you have to go back to the Scottish Highlands, to an estate where the Scots pine grows and where once lived a man with a shaggy, yellow-coated dog, who would become the forefather of them all.

TEMPERAMENT

Golden retrievers are a rare blend of intelligence, patience and sociability; it's a combination that has made them beloved companions pretty much everywhere. Their energy, especially with children, and their calm, friendly nature mean they slip easily into family life – they also get along with cats, chickens and just about anything else that shares their space. They're not guard dogs by any stretch and are far more likely to greet a stranger with affection than to see them as a threat. It would be fair to say that their big hearts are always open.

But what truly sets them apart is how attuned they are to people, which is why they've become among the most trusted therapy and assistance dogs in the world. A golden seems to know when someone needs comfort. They'll curl up next to you while you're nursing a cold, keep an eye to ensure you are okay or gently rest their head on your knee in an unfussy show of solidarity. They don't demand attention, rather they offer it. Whether it's a child struggling with anxiety, an elderly person needing company, or a family simply in need of joy, with their remarkable intuition, a golden retriever will make whatever space you're in feel like home.

Their love of people runs so deep that they don't cope well with being alone. A golden retriever left by themselves for more than two or three hours may become restless; much longer than that and they'll probably start to worry. These dogs really do want to be part of your life. When they lean their body into yours, it's as if they're saying, "Whatever you're doing, I'm coming along, too." If you're often out, consider options like family or friends calling in, dog-walking groups or services, local pet-sitting apps, or even pet camera systems. These can all help your golden feel less alone.

GROUP: Gundog.
STATUS: Secure.
ORIGIN: Developed in the 19th-century, this loveable Highlander was bred to retrieve game from both water and land, prized for its soft mouth, intelligence and trainability.
HEIGHT: Male: 56–61 cm. Female: 51–56 cm.
WEIGHT: Male: 30–34 kg. Female: 25–30 kg.

Socialisation
Friendliness
Trainability

Size

Colour

EXERCISE

Golden retrievers are a sporting breed. Bred for activity, endurance and responsiveness, most adults of this breed will need around sixty to ninety minutes of exercise daily to stay physically and mentally healthy. This might be a long walk, a swim (they're natural water dogs), a session of fetch the ball or canine sports like scent work or agility.

Puppies and seniors will need shorter sessions tailored to their energy and joint health, but all goldens benefit from mental stimulation alongside movement. An under-exercised golden may develop boredom behaviours such as chewing or barking, while the tail of a fulfilled, contented one will not stop swooshing back and forth.

TRAINING A GOLDEN

Bright, biddable and utterly devoted to their humans, golden retrievers are among the most trainable breeds in the world. They are highly responsive and a joy to work with, especially when approached with positivity and patience. Whether they're learning to navigate a busy crossing or fetching a newspaper, goldens pick up tasks quickly and carry them out with dedication.

But even the most well-mannered golden retriever starts with puppy steps, so early socialisation and consistent,

---

DID YOU KNOW? GOLDEN TRIVIA

- **Name with Meaning:** The first golden retriever, Nous, was named after the Greek word for "mind" or "intellect" – a fitting start for such a clever breed.
- **A Mark That Matters (Sometimes):** A white blaze down the nose will disqualify a golden from breed competitions like Crufts or Westminster.
- **Global Favourite:** Golden retrievers are consistently one of the top five most popular breeds in the world.
- **Home Soil:** Though they're loved worldwide, the heart of the golden retriever still beats in Scotland, where every five years, the breed is celebrated at the Guisachan Gathering, where their story began

positive reinforcement are key. As always, harsh correction can undermine trust, especially with a breed as sensitive as the golden retriever for whom that bond with their human is everything. Calm, clear communication works best. And if you mix it up with a little fun, your golden will be all in. The moment you turn a lesson into a game, their ears will be up and their tail swishing.

A well-trained golden isn't just well-behaved – they're fulfilled. These dogs are eager to learn, to help, to be included. Give them guidance, attention and love, and be prepared to receive their big old heart in return – and I promise you that adds up to a lot of love!

GROOMING & CARE

Golden retrievers turn heads with their coats that shimmer like sunlight handspun from gold silk. But with such radiant beauty comes responsibility and for first-time owners, knowing how to care for a golden's coat is essential.

Golden retrievers have a double-layered coat – the aesthetic of which is of course secondary to its function. Their soft and dense undercoat helps to regulate body temperature – keeping them toasty warm in winter and cool in the summer. Over that sits the outer coat, which is longer, flat or wavy and water-resistant – a legacy of the breed's origins in the Gàidhealtachd, where we experience extremes of weather conditions: warm, sometimes wet summers, and long, colder, wetter winters. These dogs are equipped for all eventualities!

Most goldens benefit from brushing at least twice a week and daily during moulting seasons. The quantity of fur they can leave strewn about the place is otherwise frankly unbelievable! Baths can be given every few weeks or after muddy adventures; they adore splashing, so bathtime should not be a problem! Keep an eye on their feathering too – the longer hair on their legs, tail and chest.

It's one of the breed's signature traits and gives them that storybook silhouette, but on country walks it can catch leaves, twigs and so on.

Yes, they are high-need dogs in these terms, but don't think of grooming as a chore. The moment you pause, brush out a tangle, make a fuss of them and check for brambles or dry skin is part of the bond. Grooming is time spent side by side, and your dog will most likely look forward to it – a peaceable ritual of pampering with a biscuit at the end. I'd sign up for that!

THE ORIGINS – GUISACHAN & THE GOLDEN IDEA

Dudley Marjoribanks, who would later become Lord Tweedmouth, was a man of means with a genuine love for dogs. In 1865, he acquired Nous, a yellow wavy-coated retriever, and paired him with Belle, a Tweed water spaniel – a now-extinct Scottish breed that was typically liver coloured, had a curly coat, long tail and pair of ears that hung close to the head. The pups of this union, born at the Guisachan Estate in Invernessshire, would become the foundation of a new breed – the golden retriever.

But like many good things in life,

the golden retriever came with a legend, one that began not in the Highlands, but under the striped tent of a travelling circus on the south coast of England. The story goes that Dudley was strolling the promenade in Brighton and came across a troupe of golden-coated dogs performing tricks for a seaside crowd. He was so taken by their beauty and their abilities that he bought them all, right there and then, and took them north to Guisachan, where they became the foundation of the golden retriever.

It's a brilliant story, and I can totally imagine goldens willingly adopting the role of spectacular, showstopping artistes, in fabulous costumes and playing along to the fanfare of music and a bustling, cheering crowd. The scene conjured in my mind's eye is comically theatrical – with dogs riding bikes, clowning around, jumping through hoops of fire, balancing on rolling barrels and taking bows to the roar of applause. No wonder Dudley was enchanted! It's an unexpected, delightful image – but sadly the story is completely and utterly untrue!

For decades, it made its way into books, kennels and fireside chats, and, to be fair, there's something about the golden's blend of charm and poise that makes you want to believe it. But in

1952, the myth was finally debunked. Lord Tweedmouth's great-nephew, the 6th Earl of Ilchester, discovered the original stud book – a careful record of the pairings Tweedmouth had made. His goal was clear – to create a sturdy, intelligent and trainable retriever, perfectly suited to the demands of the Highlands. A dog strong enough to work all day, gentle mouthed enough to return game undamaged and calm enough to rest quietly by the fire each evening.

So, behind the glitzy curtain, the truth is even better: what actually shaped the golden retriever wasn't dazzling showmanship with an encore of trickery. The land, weather and people of the Highlands in fact stand firmly centre stage. The golden retriever is a breed born not in the spotlight, but bred for purpose at Guisachan, nestled in those iconic pines of Glen Affric, by a man with a solid plan. Dudley was a different sort of magician; he conjured gold not quite from nothing, but from careful selection over many generations.

GOLDENS IN THE FIELD & BY THE FIRE

Originally bred as gundogs, the golden retriever was made for the field with those dense double coats that could shrug off any Highland weather with ease. Strong and steady, they could retrieve fowl from lochs and rivers, their mouths soft enough not to bruise the meat.

But even in those early days, there was a rare gentleness to them that didn't quite belong to the shooting season. And so, gradually, the golden made its way from the moor to the fireside. That breeding wasn't accidental, either. The stronger prey drive common in retrievers was carefully softened and, by the early twentieth century, they were no longer just dogs of the land. Recognised by the Kennel Club in 1913, goldens had already begun to prove they could make great companions, show champions

and be family favourites, too. Today, of course, many golden retrievers will never see a grouse or a gun. Instead, they fetch dog toys and tennis balls from gardens, and yet that original spirit – their diligence and devotion – still lives in the code tapped out in their tail beats, which naturally reads: "I love you, I love you, I love you!"

HEALTH & LONGEVITY

Golden retrievers are generally healthy, sturdy dogs, but like many other breeds, they come with a few health considerations that every prospective owner should be aware of.

The average golden lives for around ten to twelve years, though many enjoy more with the right care. A healthy, happy golden doesn't happen by accident, though. Their health and wellbeing is shaped by everyday choices – what they eat, how much they move, how they're trained and the habits you build together.

Goldens are famously fond of their food and obesity is one of the most common health issues that they might face. A balanced diet, careful portion control and regular exercise are essential to keeping your dog mobile and comfortable into old age. Slow-feeding bowls or puzzle feeders can help curb enthusiasm at mealtimes.

Among the most common inherited conditions in the breed is hip and elbow dysplasia, where the joints don't form properly, which can lead to discomfort, stiffness or arthritis later in life. Keeping your golden fit is one of the most effective ways to ease strain on the joints throughout their life. Goldens famously love the water and, just as for us humans, swimming is a wonderful, low-impact activity, which is a great option for older dogs too.

GOLDEN GATHERINGS & COMMUNITY

The Golden Retriever Club, established in 1911, is the official parent club offering guidance on health, training and responsible breeding. The Golden Retriever

Club of Scotland helps keep the breed's Highland heritage alive, while the Northern Golden Retriever Association supports owners, breeders and admirers across the north of England, offering everything from educational events to show opportunities.

These clubs protect the breed standard and welcome newcomers with the kind of warmth the dogs themselves are renowned for. Whether you're a first-time owner or a seasoned handler, there's a place for you in this extended family.

Every five years or so, there is a homecoming to the Guisachan Gathering. This is an international celebration held at the ruins of Lord Tweedmouth's estate where hundreds of dogs, and their people, arrive in a kind of golden pilgrimage to pay homage. It's a stunning celebration of thanks; more than just a meet-up, it has the energy, passion and sense of connectedness of a clan gathering.

In our ever more complex and fast-paced world, these retrievers offer a precious glimpse of simplicity. Of course, they're not perfect – they shed, they snore, they sometimes chew things they shouldn't – but they forgive quickly and love deeply, and that is surely golden.

THE GOLDEN BOY OF AULD REEKIE

In the cobbled heart of Edinburgh, where the closes run steep and the expanse of beach at Portobello is only ever a bus ride away, there lives a golden retriever who seems to glow from within. His name is Atlas – though on paper, he answers to Eyevalley Flycatcher, which sounds more like an artisanal malt whisky than a two-year-old dog. But Atlas suits him. It's a name with grandeur, brevity and – pardon the pun – direction. A name you'd give to a dog who might carry your whole world on his back, and never once complain.

Atlas belongs to Beth and Will, a young couple who share their days, their dreams and their dog with full-hearted devotion. The truth is, Atlas was part of Beth's plan long before he ever drew breath. "I had the name before I had the dog," she laughs. "I even made him an Instagram account two years before he existed." (On which you can give him a follow @atlasmackenzie . . .) She manifested him, this golden boy – and when the time came to convince Will (who, to his credit, needed no real convincing), she made her case with a full PowerPoint presentation, complete with pie charts of predicted happiness.

Two days later, as if summoned by such slideshow magic, a message arrived. A litter had been born in the Scottish Borders and there were two boys still unclaimed. They rang the breeder while standing below Edinburgh Castle – an appropriate backdrop for any life-changing decisions – and that weekend, they met the pups. Twelve tiny bundles of blond and butter, all utterly irresistible. But one wouldn't leave their side. When returned to the pen, he sat solemnly, watching them with the unmistakable look of a dog already decided. He'd chosen his people, and they named him Atlas on the spot.

Now two years old and weighing in at a stately forty-five kilograms, Atlas lives a life that's part city slicker, part seaside wanderer. He stretches out under pub benches in Leith, chases foam at Portobello beach and draws a crowd without ever meaning to. He has what you'd call presence – that rare, luminous quality that makes strangers soften and smile as he passes.

But he's no diva. Atlas is gentle to the bone. Despite early warnings of chewed cushions and shredded toys, he's never destroyed a thing. His first toy – a wee green crocodile – is still intact, though it's had more baths than your rubber duckie. His most prized possession, however, is a massive dog teddy, which he treats like a pup of his own. He carries it carefully from room to room, soft and solemn, like he's bearing a secret.

Beth and Will both grew up with dogs, especially collies. Will's family on the Black Isle bred and showed rough collies across the UK, including at Crufts. And there's a golden thread running through their story, too: a relative of Will's once worked at Guisachan. That Atlas, with his honeyed coat and kindly eyes, should find his way into Will's life feels a little like fate, like a breed returning, in some small way, to kin.

Atlas is never far from his humans. He joins them at cafés, tags along to pub quizzes, even accompanies them to work. As Beth says, they don't bring him into their world: he brings them into his. And earlier this year, when Beth and Will tied the knot, there's no doubt who was the guest of honour. Tail high, head proud, Atlas was there beside them as they said their vows on the Ayrshire coast with Ailsa Craig in the distance; he's a golden ribbon in their love story.

If you had to sum up Atlas, you might say he's the dog you imagine when you close your eyes and wish hard enough. But for Beth and Will, no such summing-up is needed. He's their once-in-a-lifetime dog – and all three of them know how lucky they are.

THE GOLDEN GIRLS

It was early when we met by the sea, hoping for soft morning light and perhaps a swim. But the weather had other plans; a sky like pewter and sheets of rain coming in sideways – smirry, dense and relentless – soaking through everything without ceremony. Still, my friend Eileen arrived without complaint, two goldens at her side and a wee smile on her face.

Caorann and Nell were bred by Sylvia Baird of Drumtochty in Perthshire. Caorann, now nearly ten, is the thoughtful one – calm and watchful, with the wisdom of years well lived. Nell, five, is brighter in spirit – lively, affectionate and always the first to find the joy in things. Their Kennel Club names – Drumtochty Caorann and Drumtochty Destiny – suit them perfectly.

Caorann was once part of a larger household of dogs, but when her older companions passed, the quiet was too much. Eileen reached out to Sylvia, asking if any goldens might be in need of a home – and found there was one; a young female whose owner was downsizing. That dog turned out to be Nell, from a litter Sylvia had once offered to Eileen when she wasn't in a position to say yes. This time, the answer was clear. "She must have been meant to come," Eileen says. "Destiny, after all."

Now, the two are inseparable: Caorann brings the steadiness and Nell brings the spark. They share soft toys between them – never torn, never chewed – and an unspoken, sisterly rhythm. On walks, they move in step. At home, they curl together like pieces of a jigsaw puzzle.

That wild morning on the Argyll coast, they seemed completely unbothered by the rain. Where the humans huddled into their hoods, the dogs stood proudly in the bracken, rain catching on their whiskers, the hills rising behind them. They were all the more golden for the grey day, and with girls like these for pals, it's hard not to feel blessed. All I can say is, thank you for being a friend.

Cha truagh leam cù 's marag m'a amhaich.
I don't pity a dog with a black pudding round his neck.

THE HEBRIDEAN BAKER'S OATY DOG BISCUITS
For the best dogs in Scotland!

Through the years, Coinneach has been frequently asked to create dog treats, but it wasn't until we started feeding our own dogs a mixture of raw and fresh food that he devised this recipe. They are hearty, healthy and we know exactly what's in them. For dogs, as for humans, the motto rings true – *homemade is always best*. These oaty dog biscuits are packed with natural goodness, free from artificial ingredients and are the perfect treat to say "mòran taing" to the dogs who enrich our lives.

INGREDIENTS
(Makes a generous batch)
200 g rolled oats
150 g wholemeal flour
1 carrot (boiled and mashed)
1 egg
1 tablespoon natural peanut butter (salt and xylitol free)
2 tablespoons cold-pressed rapeseed oil
100 ml Karnlea Beef Bone Broth – for Dogs & Cats
A small pinch of dried parsley

METHOD
In a mixing bowl, combine the oats, flour and parsley.

Add the mashed carrot, egg, peanut butter and oil. Mix well until the ingredients come together.

Gradually add the bone broth to form a firm but pliable dough. If it's too dry, add a little extra broth.

Roll out the dough on a floured surface to about ½ cm thick (approx. ¼ inch). Use your favourite cutter or hand chop into bite-sized pieces.

Place them on a greaseproof paper-lined tray and bake in a preheated oven at 160°C fan / 350°F for 25 to 30 minutes, until golden and crisp.

Allow them to cool completely before offering one to your four-legged friend.

STORAGE
Once cooled, store in an airtight container for one week. They can also be frozen for up to three months; you will need to defrost before serving.

FEEDING AS NATURE INTENDED

THE BENEFITS OF A RAW DIET FOR DOGS

Long before tinned meat and huge sacks of kibble, dogs shared fires with us, eating what we ate – or what we couldn't. From the Highland bothy to the Borders farm, their diet was shaped by nature, scraps and survival. They gnawed on bones tossed from the kitchen door, scavenged game from the hill and thrived on the leftovers of rural life.

Today, as more owners feed their dogs with the same care they'd take over a family meal, a revolution is taking place in kitchens and kennels across the country – a return to raw. Raw feeding isn't about trends, it's about trust. Trust in the dog's body, in common sense and in the idea that what's fresh and real might well be best. To some it may seem strange or offputtingly messy. But to others, it makes nutritional and financial sense: you know what's going into the dog's bowl and you know why.

A DIET WRITTEN IN THEIR BONES

Despite thousands of years at our side, dogs remain biologically close to their wild ancestors. Whether a sighthound, terrier, scent dog or herder, their teeth are shaped for tearing flesh, their stomachs capable of digesting uncooked meat and bone with ease. Their short, acidic and efficient digestive track was not built for grains or biscuits, but for prey. Wolves, cousins to every dog on the sofa, thrive on whole carcasses – muscle, bone, organs, skin, fur and all. Our dogs might now sleep indoors and wear raincoats in November, but the physiology of their bodies haven't changed all that much.

WHAT'S WRONG WITH KIBBLE?

Processed dog food became popular in the mid-twentieth century because it was cheap, shelf-stable and marketed as complete. But many commercial brands are cooked at high temperatures that destroy nutrients, and they rely heavily on fillers like maize, rice and synthetic additives that don't belong in a canine diet. The result?

- Obesity from excess carbs.
- Itchy skin and upset stomachs from artificial preservatives.
- Dental decay from soft or starchy foods.
- Dogs who are constantly hungry, tired or just "off".

For some dogs, it's true that kibble works, but for many, it's like feeding a coyote on cornflakes.

RAW BONES – REALLY?

Yes! Raw bones are not only safe, but essential – when fed appropriately. Cooked bones are dangerous: they splinter, dry out and can cause serious harm. But raw chicken wings, lamb ribs or duck necks are soft, pliable and packed with calcium and phosphorus. Chewing them supports dental health, strengthens the jaw and satisfies natural instincts. Many butchers will happily give you bones for the dog: it is well worth asking. A balanced raw diet includes about 10 per cent bone content, so feeding dogs these smaller, easier to swallow bones will mean that there is not an old bone left lying around or stashed under the sofa.

THE RAW DEAL

Scientific studies on the following benefits are still taking place, but the anecdotal evidence from owners is compelling. Many report that feeding their dogs a raw and fresh diet offers a different path, with:

- Firmer, smaller poos.
- Glossy coats and healthy skin.
- Cleaner teeth and fresher breath.
- Improved gut health.
- More energy and better mood.
- Lean muscle and proper weight.
- Fewer vet visits.

WHAT GOES IN THE BOWL?

A typical raw meal might include:
- Muscle meat – beef, chicken, lamb, venison or fish (heart counts as muscle).
- Organ meat – liver, kidney, spleen (rich in nutrients).
- Raw meaty bones – wings, ribs, necks.
- Raw eggs.
- Optional vegetables and fruit – leafy greens, carrots, berries.
- Supplements (if needed) – fish oil, kelp, probiotics.

SO WHAT DO I NEED TO DO?

Some owners prepare meals from scratch. Others use pre-made frozen meals – convenient and widely available, albeit expensive. Start them young if you can. Puppies raised on raw tend to thrive, and you don't necessarily need to continue with it long term. For all dogs, at whatever stage, even if you don't feed raw (or fresh) full-time, adding some fresh food helps. This can be a raw egg, a bit of veg, some fresh lightly cooked meat or offcuts from your butcher. Raw or fresh doesn't need to be perfect – just real.

> ### DID YOU KNOW?
> A dog's stomach acid can reach a pH as low as 1. This powerful digestive system helps dogs break down raw bones safely and neutralise bacteria.

RAW & REAL

Ask your butcher for scraps and offcuts; if you are buying meat from them, then they'll usually be happy to oblige – and freebies are always good. Remember, any step towards fresh food is a step in the right direction – for dogs as for humans! It's true that feeding raw isn't always tidy and there's freezer space to consider. But there's also satisfaction in feeding something real to your dog. I guarantee you will notice a shine in the coat, a gleam in the eyes, and all the benefits for a dog that feels more alive.

CHOOSING WHAT'S RIGHT FOR YOUR DOG

Raw feeding isn't for everyone – and that's fine. Every dog, every home and every owner is different. What matters most is feeding your dog well, with care and curiosity – not just out of habit and not just because the label claims it's best. The pet food industry is a multibillion-dollar machine, but branding isn't biology. Just as you would with your own food, look beyond the slogans, read the label and ask yourself questions.

You don't have to go raw to feed well; some gently cooked or cold-pressed foods are excellent. Some kibbles, too. But adding a little fresh food – whatever you can manage – will make a difference. In the end, what matters is that your dog is thriving – and that you feel confident to make the choices that work for you both.

CÙ MATH! GUID DUG! TEACHING YOUR DOG SCOTLAND'S LANGUAGES

Fàilte! Welcome! Whether it's Gaelic or Scots, teaching your dog commands in one of our native languages is a wonderful way to connect with heritage while strengthening the bond with your canine companion. Gaelic has echoed through Scotland's glens for over a thousand years and many of our traditional dog breeds – like the Westie, Skye terrier and Scottish deerhound – will historically have heard Gaelic naturally through the ages. Scots, too, has a long history in working dog life, where regional varieties like Lallan Scots, the Doric of the northeast and the Shetland dialect each carry their own rich vocabulary that would have been familiar to the ears of Dandies, Scotties and Shetland sheepdogs.

Dogs learn through sound, tone and repetition, so using Gaelic or Scots commands is just as easy as English and – let's be honest – your dog is the perfect, judgement-free partner for practising new languages. No need to fear getting it wrong or sounding silly. Speaking aloud in Gaelic or Scots with your dog can build confidence, explore rhythm and pronunciation and help you both to embrace these languages as living, spoken parts of everyday life.

HOW TO BEGIN

- **Start With the Basics** – Pick a few key commands and use them consistently.
- **Mind Your Pronunciation** – Keep it clear and distinct so your dog learns quickly.
- **Use Hand Signals** – Gestures reinforce spoken commands.
- **Praise Often** – Whether it's treats, a belly rub or a cheerful *Cù math!* or *Guid dug!* always reward good behaviour.
- **Short and Sweet** – Keep training sessions to five to ten minutes so your dog stays engaged.

WHY TRAIN YOUR DOG IN GAELIC AND SCOTS?

Cultural Connection: Keep Scotland's languages active in daily life.

Stronger Bond: Learning together builds trust, especially in the language of our ancestors.

It's Fun, Aye! Nothing raises a smile like hearing a dug mind its manners in Scots or Gaelic.

COMMON COMMANDS IN GAELIC AND SCOTS

ENGLISH	GAELIC	SOUND IT OUT	SCOTS	SOUND IT OUT
Sit	Suidh sìos	Soo-ee shee-us	Sit doon	Sit doon
Stay	Fuirich	Foo-rikh	Bide	By-de
Lie down	Laigh sìos	Lay shee-us	Lie doon	Lie doon
Come	Trobhad	Tro-wat	Come	Cum
Heel	Ri mo thaobh	Ree mo hoov	In aboot	Inaboot
Leave it	Fàg e	Faag-eh	Lae' it!	Lee-it
Drop it	Leig às	Lekh ass	Drap it	Drap-it
Good dog	Cù math	Koo maah	Guid dug	Gwid dug
Good boy	Balach math	Bal-ukh maah	Guid loon	Gwid loon
Good girl	Caileag mhath	Kal-ak vah	Guid lass	Gwid lass
No / Stop	Sguir	Skoor	Nae	Nay
Quiet	Bi sàmhach	Bee sah-vakh	Wheesht	Wheesht
Fetch	Tog e	Tok-eh	Feetch it	Feetch it
Get down	Thalla sìos	Hal-a shee-us	Get doon	Get doon
Here	Seo	Shaw	Hai	Ha-ye
Walk	Cuairt	Koo-arsht	Waukies	Waw-kees
Bed	Leabaidh	Leh-bee	In yer kip	In yer kip
Good for you	Sin thu fhèin	Shin oo hey-n	Oan yersel	Oan yersel

A LANGUAGE FOR LIFE

Want to go further?
- For Gaelic check out **SpeakGaelic.scot**
- For Scots visit **ScotsLanguage.com** or explore **ShetlandDialect.org.uk**

Of course, the very best way to learn is to come and immerse yourself and your canine chum: walk the glens, chat with folk and let the dogs of Scotland show you the way.

WHAT'S IN A NAME?
SCOTTISH NAMES FOR YOUR DOG

Choosing a name is one of the joys of welcoming a dog into your life – and what better way to celebrate their heritage (or yours) than with a name steeped in Scottish culture?

MALE NAMES

NAME	MEANING
Angus	Noble strength, a name for kings and clans
Arran	Island beauty, like a Scotland in miniature
Balach (Bah-lukh)	Gaelic for "boy", simple and spirited
Bran	Name of Fionn's dog
Calum	Peaceful dove, calm and companionable
Cuilean (Koo-len)	Gaelic for "puppy", perfect for the wee yin
Dìleas (Gee-lass)	Faithful and loyal, the heart of a true companion
Donald	Proud chief, a timeless Highland name
Dougal	Dark stranger, rich with clan legacy
Dug	A cheeky Scots nod to the dog itself
Eachan (Eh-khən)	Little horse, strong and swift
Fergus	Man of strength, noble and bold
Fionn (Fyun)	Fair one, Gaelic hero
Ghillie	A loyal guide on hill or riverbank
Hamish	James in Highland dress, hearty and dependable
Harris	Windswept and rugged, like the island itself
Hector	Steadfast hero, brave and noble
Lachlan	Warrior from the lochs, full of ancient depth
Laochan (Loo-kh-an)	Wee hero
Laddie	The wee fellow in your life
Lewis	A Hebridean treasure
Mac	"Son of", central to clan naming
Mirk	Old Scots for darkness or mist, mysterious and moody
Rabbie	After Burns himself, bard of the people
Rìgh (Ree)	King
Ruairidh (Roo-uh-ree)	Gaelic for Rory, the red-haired king
Seòras (Shoh-ris)	George in Gaelic, strong and stately

NAME	MEANING
Seumas (Shay-mus)	James, dignified and true
Tam	For Tam o' Shanter, a name that gallops with spirit
Tormod	Norse-rooted, bold and enduring
Wallace	Freedom's son, a name of fierce pride
Wullie	Everyman's William, cheeky and warm

FEMALE NAMES

NAME	MEANING
Ailsa	From Ailsa Craig, an island rock in the Firth of Clyde
Beathag (Beh-ak)	Beth in Gaelic, full of spark
Bellag	Affectionate diminutive of Bella
Bonnie	Beautiful and bright, a classic Scots endearment
Brèagha (Bree-uh)	Beautiful in Gaelic, lyrical and light
Brìde (Bree-juh)	Exalted one, flame of spring, guardian of hearth and healing
Caileag (Kal-ak)	Gaelic for "girl", sweet and simple
Eilidh (Ay-lee)	Sunbeam through mist, radiant and soft
Flòraidh (Flaw-ree)	For Flora MacDonald, brave and beloved
Heather	Hardy and graceful, like the bloom on Highland hills
Iona	Sacred island of peace and poetry
Islay	Elegant island name, smooth and soulful
Jeannie	A Scottish gem, soft and timeless
Katie	Friendly and familiar, the girl in the next glen
Lassie	The perfect name for a wee girl
Morag	Great and splendid, a matriarchal classic
Màiri (Mah-ree)	Gaelic for Mary, gentle and enduring
Mairead (My-rud)	Pearl of the Highlands
Peigi (Peh-gee)	Gaelic for Peggy, full of charm
Sadie	Sweet and strong, with old-fashioned sparkle
Seònaid (Shoh-nitch)	Gaelic for Janet, refined and rich in heritage
Shuna	A quiet island name, soft on the tongue
Sìne (Shee-nuh)	Gaelic for Jean, strong and steady
Sorcha (Sor-uh-kha)	Bright one, clear and true
Ùna (Oo-nuh)	Gentle one, delicate yet deep

SUITABLE FOR ANY DOG

NAME	MEANING
Bàrd (Baa-rst)	A poet
Beinn	Gaelic for mountain, strong and grounded
Blether	A talkative companion, full of stories
Braw	Handsome or excellent, a proper compliment
Broch	Ancient stone dwelling, enduring and proud
Ceòl (key-ol)	Music
Clyde	Glasgow's iconic river
Coorie	To snuggle, or cuddle
Daftie	The silly one
Dannsair	A dancer
Dram	A nip of whisky
Dreich	A moody day, perfect for a brooding pup
Dun	Fort or hill, sturdy and earthy
Firth	Where land and sea embrace, calm and sure
Gallus	Cheeky, mischievous or bold
Inver	At the river's mouth, great for a water dog
Jura	Wild and free, quietly powerful
Kelpie	Water spirit of legend, untamed and clever
Lochy	Loch-lovely, cool and calm
Luath (Loo-ah)	Fast of foot, the quick one
Mull	Land of mists and music
Ness	From Loch Ness, mysterious and bold
Nevis	Highest peak, lofty and grand
Oban	Gateway to the isles, warm and welcoming
Oran	Little song, or saintly soul
Orkney	Norse-tinged and ocean-strong
Peat	Rich and earthy, full of character
Peerie	Small or tiny in Shetland dialect
Skye	Island of dreams, dramatic and beloved
Tay	River deep, quietly wise
Tiree	Sunshine isle, breezy and bright
Tobermory	An island village of character

SCOTLAND'S DOGS ON SHOW

As we've seen in our chat about feeding your dog, in the good old days, dogs were likely to be fed kitchen scraps or whatever could be spared as a dog's dinner. Some historical accounts mention "dog bread" or "hound loaves" baked on estates or in the communities, but these were low-key and rustic, certainly not commercial in any modern sense.

In 1860, at the Liverpool docks, an American entrepreneur named James Spratt was watching stray dogs scavenging for hardtack – the dry, durable biscuit eaten by sailors – when inspiration stuck him. He would set about creating a cookie for canines, a baked blend of meat, veg and cereal bound into what he'd call the Meat Fibrine Dog Cake. It was the first commercial dog biscuit: branded, marketed, somewhat nutritious and aimed squarely at sporting gentlemen with dogs. Spratt's innovation laid the foundation for the pet food industry, and his company became the first to manufacture dog biscuits on a global scale. Within a few decades, the humble treat had become a marker of care, class awareness and modern dog-keeping.

And then Charlie stepped into the story.

In 1865, at the age of thirteen, a bright-eyed lad named Charles began work at Spratt's as an errand boy. He'd sweep floors, fetch ledgers and watch the business world with sharp interest. He had a head for enterprise and an instinct for the job, and, over time, he climbed the ranks to become general manager. His role took him across Europe, selling biscuits not just to dog owners, but to breeders, clubs and aristocrats. He understood that dogs were no longer mere workers or guards – they were companions, champions and showpieces.

Fortune would have it that Charlie's career was rising just as the fashion for pedigree breeding and dog showing was gaining ground. In 1859, Britain saw its first organised dog show, held in Newcastle and featuring sixty gundogs. Enthusiasm for competition quickly grew, and in 1873, the Kennel Club was formed – the world's first national registry, created to bring order to an increasingly competitive and, at times, chaotic show scene.

THE SCOTTISH KENNEL CLUB

Founded in 1881, this is Scotland's oldest active canine organisation and one of the longest-running kennel clubs worldwide. From its early exhibitions – held in Edinburgh and Glasgow – to today's flagship May championship shows at the Royal Highland Centre, it has long celebrated Scotland's breeds. These shows remain the largest in Scotland, showcasing conformation standards and supporting broader goals like canine welfare, breeder and owner education, and youth engagement.

SPOTLIGHT – THE SCOTTISH BREEDS CANINE CLUB

Founded in 1971 to specifically champion Scotland's native breeds, the club remains the beating heart of our canine heritage. Their annual Championship Show – held each spring at Lanark – is the only UK event dedicated exclusively to Scottish dogs, and it celebrates conformation, character and cultural legacy in equal measure. Not only is the show a great day out, but it's also a brilliant place to start if you're looking to see these dogs up close, connect with breed clubs, or meet owners and reputable breeders passionate about preserving Scotland's canine traditions.

FROM BISCUIT TO BEST IN SHOW

Young Charlie foresaw all this unfolding – the passion, the prestige, the public appetite – and he was paying close, entrepreneurial attention. His travels had taken him from London to Paris, from the show grounds of Brussels to the drawing rooms of Berlin, and in all these places he had met kennel masters, duchesses, gamekeepers and gentlemen breeders. He watched how different nations paraded their canine pride on a lead, how a well-groomed hound could reflect status, taste, a chosen aesthetic or even national character. He attended shows, judged entries, negotiated supply deals and always took note of what drew a crowd, what stirred admiration, and he saw what was needed. Charlie understood that dog shows weren't just exhibitions – they were theatre.

So in 1891, he staged a new kind of event – a grand showcase of dogs and dogdom that brought together breeders, aristocrats, traders and the curious public under one spectacular roof – and he gave it his own name. Cruft.

Legacy has to start somewhere and this is surely a great origin story! Cruft's

Greatest Dog Show was born and grew into the most prestigious celebration of pedigree dogs in the world, a show that outlasted its founder, his biscuits and its original venue because as every dog lover knows, a good name sticks.

CRUFTS - A BRITISH LEGACY OF CANINE EXCELLENCE

After its glittering debut in 1891, Crufts quickly became an institution. Under Charles Cruft's watchful eye, it blossomed into something grand – a celebration of pedigree, presentation and public spectacle. In that first year, over 2,400 entries were registered across thirty-six breeds. While comprehensive records of all participating dogs are limited, documentation shows that the rough collie was among the Scottish breeds present at the inaugural show, entered by none other than Queen Victoria herself. Called Darnley II, he secured fourth place in the Open Dog class.

For many years, the highest accolade was the title of "Best Champion". But in 1928, something new was introduced. "Best in Show" was an honour that has since become the holy grail of the show world. The first dog to claim it? A sleek and "faultless" blue greyhound girl – kept by an eccentric zoo owner, no less – named Primley Sceptre. The following year, the coveted title went to

---

SCOTTISH BREED BEST IN SHOW WINNERS AT CRUFTS

Scottish Terrier
The Scottish terrier made history as the first Crufts Best in Show winner under its current format.
- 1929 – Heather Necessity; owned by Mr Robert Chapman, she paved the way for generations of Scotties to come.
- 2015 – McVan's To Russia With Love.

West Highland White Terrier
The Westie has captured the top title three times across the decades.
- 1976 – Dianthus Buttons.
- 1990 – Olac Moon Pilot.
- 2016 – Burneze Geordie Girl.

Bearded Collie
A Beardie bounced us out of the 1980s by taking the top spot.
- 1989 – Potterdale Classic of Moonhill.

Westminster Kennel Club Dog Show is one of the oldest continuous sporting events in the United States, outpaced only by the Kentucky Derby. It began in Manhattan, founded by a group of gentlemen sportsmen who first gathered to compare their pointers and setters at the bar of the Westminster Hotel.

The inaugural show drew over 1,200 entries and quickly captured the American imagination. Among the early entries were several Scottish breeds. The Scottish terrier found favour early at Westminster, admired for its tenacity and distinctive outline. The Dandie Dinmont terrier, with its unique shape and literary pedigree, was also exhibited in these formative years. Though precise breed records from the 1877 show are scarce, early catalogues from the 1880s confirm growing participation of these and other Scottish dogs, such as the rough collie and Gordon setter. Their presence helped shape international appreciation for Scotland's native breeds long before they reached superstardom in other show rings.

From the start, the Westminster event was wrapped in the velvet of high society – attended by tycoons, statesmen and celebrities alike. Today, nearly two hundred AKC-recognised breeds compete each year, each vying for a place in the annals of American dog history. If Crufts is the royal pageant of canine circles,

a dog with rather shorter legs but no less stature. Heather Necessity, a spirited wee Scottish terrier, became the first of Scotland's native breeds to win the coveted Best in Show at Crufts.

And so, what began with a biscuit is now a cultural institution. Crufts has become a landmark celebration of the bond between people and dogs; its legacy a living history of how we choose, breed and adore our canine companions.

WESTMINSTER – AMERICA'S DOG SHOW

Across the Atlantic, another dog show was making its mark. Established in 1877 – fourteen years before Crufts – the

Westminster is its Broadway premiere – glamorous, iconic and full of the swagger of champions.

WHY IT MATTERS

These moments of visibility and triumph are symbols of perseverance, breed identity and dignity. Each win represents the passion, dedication and commitment of owners, handlers and clubs. The global exposure that these accolades bestow upon a breed is exceptional, and they represent a flame of hope for the breeds still waiting for their day in the sun.

SCOTTISH BREED BEST IN SHOW WINNERS AT WESTMINSTER

Scotland's native breeds have truly made their mark at America's most prestigious dog show, where they have not only competed but triumphed.

Scottish Terrier
With eight Best in Show titles, the Scottish terrier ranks among the most successful breeds in Westminster history.
- 1911 – Tickle Em Jock.
- 1945 – Shieling's Signature.
- 1950 – Walsing Winning Trick of Edgerstoune.
- 1965 – Carmichaels Fanfare.
- 1967 – Bardene Bingo.
- 1985 – Braeburn's Close Encounter.
- 1994 – Bardene Bingo.
- 1995 – Gaelforce Post Script.
- 2010 – Roundtown Mercedes of Maryscot.

West Highland White Terrier
A breed known for its charisma and confidence, the Westie has twice taken home the top honours at Westminster.
- 1942 – Wolvey Pattern of Edgerstoune.
- 1962 – Elfinbrook Simon.

Skye Terrier
The rare and dignified Skye terrier has also stood at the pinnacle of the American dog show.
- 1969 – Glamoor Good News.

Rough Collie
The rough collie made its Westminster breakthrough in the early years of the show.
- 1929 – Laund Loyalty of Bellhaven.

Scottish Deerhound
When this Scottish deerhound was the first of its breed to take Best in Show, she won hearts across America.
- 2011 – Foxcliffe Hickory Wind.

SCOTTISH BREED CLUBS & ASSOCIATIONS

Here is a selection of clubs supporting Scotland's native dog breeds. These organisations promote breed health, heritage and responsible ownership. Contact them directly for more information, and I assure you there'll be a warm welcome awaiting you.

CLUB NAME	CONTACT/ WEBSITE
Caledonian Dandie Dinmont Terrier Club	caledoniandandies.com
Southern Dandie Dinmont Terrier Club	southerndandies.com
Dandie Dinmont Terrier Club	ddtc.co.uk
Scottie Club UK	scottieclub.uk
West Highland White Terrier Club	thewesthighlandwhiteterrierclub.co.uk
Westie Rescue Scheme	westierescuescheme.org.uk
Skye Terrier Club	skyeterrierclub.org.uk
Cairn Terrier Club of Scotland	thecairnterrierclub.co.uk
Border Terrier Club	theborderterrierclub.co.uk
Bearded Collie Club	beardedcollieclub.co.uk
Golden Retriever Club	thegoldenretrieverclub.co.uk
Golden Retriever Club of Scotland	goldenretrieverclubofscotland.com
Border Collie Club of Great Britain	bordercollieclub.com
Rough Collie Breed Council	roughcolliebreedcouncil.co.uk
Scottish Collie Club	scottishcollieclub.com
Smooth Collie Club of Great Britain	smoothcollieclubofgb.co.uk
Scottish Shetland Sheepdog Club	scottish-sheltie.org.uk
Gordon Setter Club of Scotland	gordonsetterclubofscotland.co.uk
British Gordon Setter Club	britishgordonsetterclub.co.uk
The Deerhound Club	deerhound.co.uk
Scottish Breeds Canine Club	scottishbreeds.co.uk
The Kennel Club	thekennelclub.org.uk/getting-a-dog/are-you-ready/breed-rescue

CEUD MÌLE TAING / A HUNDRED THOUSAND THANKS

It takes a village to produce a book. Heartfelt thanks to the wider pack of people and pooches who brought this one to life – none of it could have happened without you!

To the team at Black & White – Ali, Thomas, Tonje (tusen takk min hundekjære venn!), Rachel, Hannah, Lizzie and Clem. Thank you for giving Scotland's native breeds a bookish moment in the sun. Special thanks to my wonderful editor Emma Hargrave.

All the love to our photographer Susie Lowe – equal parts artist and dog-whisperer. Your photos sing – and sharing the road with you and Machrie was braw!

Mum, Dad, Uncle Stuart, and my brothers Mark & Robin – thank you for always supporting me. Mary Anne MacDonald, Màiri, Eilidh & Màiri bheag, Faye MacLean, Rhona MacInnes, Marion Govig and Maureen Flip. Katrina and Rosemary Inkster. Clan MacDougall and the Dunollie Preservation Trust, Fiona MacLeod, Gavin Hopkins, Izzy Law, Alan MacMillan, Kaylee Williamson, Lauren O'Connell, Kelly Ann Thomson, Polly Pullar, my colleagues at BBC Alba and Storyboard Studios – tapa leibh air fad.

To the amazing humans who live with, champion and care so deeply for our native breeds. You are their ambassadors every single day, and knowing you fills me with hope for these dogs.

Murdo MacLeod, Brodie, Riley and Harvey, Rhona and Paul McGuire, Stan and Jess, Joanna Maclean, Effie Bheag, Stella McIver, Rosie and Isla, Paul Killen and Stephen Campbell, Gio and Florence, Norman Martin, Hamish, Ian Dyer and Brian Whitney, Skye, Ali Cox and Angie Miller, Sissy, Thelma and Morty, Claudia Massie, Magnus and Tibbie, Eileen Sinclair, Nell and Caorann, Sheila McGregor and the Collies of Slaterich Farm, Ceitidh Alice Galbraith and Cameron, Isbean, Sgadan and Jock, Jean Senior, Arwen and Thyra, Sheila Sharp, Torrin and Faolin, Anne McAlpine, Laika, Angie Macfarlane, Fergus and Katie Morag, Catriona Stewart and Peter Sadowski, Morar, John and Linda Scott, Roag, Eleanor Bartlett, Vaila, Karen Scott and Oskar, Chrisanne Brown and Marley, James Gray and Kirsten Johnston, Anam, Christine and Tom Clark, Shian, Luing and Nave, Christina and Calum MacAulay, Fergus, Seumas and Magnus, Beth and Will MacKenzie, Atlas, Mark Shaw, Ghillie, Olwen and Kevin King, Brèagha and Sula, Fliss and Nick Hopkins, Radley, Fergus, Brodie, Hamish, Dougal and wee Effie, Tanya Houston, Mac and Jeff, Heather Graveson and Peggy, Milly and Scott Robertson, Ghillie, Heather Young, Harris, Emma Scott, Stevie, Isa, Tom Ramsay and Holly McAllister, Ruby, Andy and Bridgit Findlay, Archie and Fergus, Carol Doherty and Rab Robertson, Lyle, Neil MacDonald, Bella and Tessie, Mari Hamilton, Wyvis, Edal, Clova and Darcie, Kelly Crawford, Rodney and last but not least, Esme Rennie for bringing the Rain!

Coinneach, for always making things better, and of course Peigi and Flòraidh, for faithfully accompanying me under the desk throughout this process.

ABOUT THE AUTHOR

Peter MacQueen is a Scottish television presenter, producer and author with a lifelong love of the great outdoors. Born on Scotland's west coast, he has gone on to share adventures with audiences of all ages, creating inspiring documentaries and series for BBC Alba, Channel 4 and CBBC. He is best known as the host of the Gaelic series *Cù Leis Thu?* and *Gàrradh Phàdruig*.

His first book, *The Art of Hutting*, celebrates the joys of off-grid living and reconnecting with nature. Peter now lives near Oban with his partner – bestselling author and baker Coinneach MacLeod – along with their Westie Flòraidh and Peigi the Dandie Dinmont terrier. Together, they are developing a new agritourism croft business where food, folklore and four-legged friends come together to offer guests a true taste of Scotland.

Follow Peter on Instagram
@highlandhutter

PHOTO CREDITS

All photos © Peter MacQueen, other than those on the pages listed below:

Susie Lowe: iv, 2, 6, 14, 18, 20, 24, 25, 28, 30, 34, 36, 39, 40, 41, 42, 44, 48, 52, 53, 56, 58, 60, 61, 66, 69, 71, 74, 75, 76, 80, 83, 84, 86, 88, 90, 99, 102, 103, 104, 107, 112, 114, 117, 119, 121, 122, 126, 128, 130, 131, 133, 134, 136, 138, 143, 145, 146, 147, 148, 149, 151, 152, 154, 159, 160, 165, 167, 172, 178, 180, 182, 193, 198, 200, 202, 204, 207, 208, 209, 214, 216, 218, 220, 221, 222, 223, 224, 225, 230, Endpaper.

Stewart Attwood Photography for the Game & Wildlife Coservation Trust Scottish Game Fair: 26; **Alan MacMillan:** 100; **Claudia Massie:** 106; **Adobe Stock:** 108, 242, 244; **Esme Rennie:** 163, 168, 175, 177, 179; **Lauren O'Connell:** 191, 246; **Kaylee Williamson:** 187, 188, 189; **Polly Pullar:** 194; **Julian Davies (SARDA Scotland):** 203; **Kelly Ann Thomson:** 210, 217, 219; **Isabelle Law Photography:** 226; **Gavin Hopkins:** 228.